WESTWARD
Ho!

John Wesley Powell, one of the greatest explorers of the West, made his first voyage down the Colorado River in 1869. This image, entitled *Running a Rapid*, shows the thrill and the danger Powell and his brave men faced.

WESTWARD HO!

ELEVEN EXPLORERS
OF THE WEST

BY CHARLOTTE
FOLTZ JONES

HOLIDAY HOUSE / *New York*

DEDICATED TO

BILL C. R. JONES

who shares the fascination

of the West

ACKNOWLEDGMENTS

The author wishes to acknowledge the assistance of: Mary Cash, Holiday House; Kathleen Cassaday, Boulder Public Library; Dr. Haworth Clover, Jedediah Smith Society; Staff of the Clymer Museum of Art; Bonnie Coles, Library of Congress; Staff of the Colorado Historical Society; Robert S. Cox, American Philosophical Society; Staff of the Denver Public Library, Western History Department; Judith Hosafros, Wyoming Game and Fish Department; Colleen Hyde, Grand Canyon National Park; Staff of the Independence National Historical Park; Susan Camilleri Konar, Vancouver Public Library; Sandra Lowry, Fort Laramie National Historic Site; Joe McGregor, U.S. Geological Survey; Larry K. Mensching, Joslyn Art Museum; Daryl Morrison, University of the Pacific Libraries; Staff of the National Archives and Records Administration; Staff of the National Archives of Canada; Staff of the Oregon State Legislative Administration; David Pearson, Columbia River Maritime Museum; Staff of the Utah State Historical Society; Chad Wall, Nebraska State Historical Society; Staff of the Wyoming State Archives; Staff of the Yellowstone National Park Photo Archives; Staff of the Yosemite Museum, Yosemite National Park.

Library of Congress Cataloging-in-Publication Data
Jones, Charlotte Foltz.
Westward ho! : eleven explorers of the West / Charlotte Foltz Jones.
p. cm.
Summary: A collective biography of eleven men who explored the West in the 18th and 19th centuries,
including ship's officers, fur traders, and Army officers.
Includes bibliographical references (p. 210) and index.
Contents: Robert Gray (1755–1806)—George Vancouver (1757–1798)—Alexander Mackenzie (1764–1820)—
John Colter (1774 or 1775–1813)—Zebulon Montgomery Pike (1779–1813)—Stephen Harriman Long (1784–1864)—
James Bridger (1804–1881)—Jedediah Strong Smith (1799–1831)—Joseph Reddeford Walker (1798–1876)—
John C. Fremont (1813–1890)—John Wesley Powell (1834–1902).
ISBN 0-8234-1586-4
1. Explorers—West (U.S.)—Biography—Juvenile literature.   2. Pioneers—West (U.S.)—Biography—Juvenile literature.
3. West (U.S.)—Biography—Juvenile literature   4. West (U.S.)—Discovery and exploration—Juvenile literature.
5. West (U.S.)—History—Juvenile literature.   6. Frontier and pioneer life—West (U.S.)—Juvenile literature.
[1. Explorers. 2. Pioneers.   3. West (U.S.)—Biography.   4. West (U.S.)—Discovery and exploration.
5. West (U.S.)—History. 6. Frontier and pioneer life—West (U.S.)]   I. Title
F590.5.J66 2004
910'.92'2—dc22
2003057004

CONTENTS

INTRODUCTION

❖─══◎══─❖

E xplorers.

Sometimes an "explorer" is a person who discovers something for the very first time . . . something that has never been discovered before.

But that's not always true. A person can explore a mountain, a seashore, or even an amusement park. That doesn't mean they are the very *first* to explore that site. Anyone can "discover" a restaurant or a park or even a new route to the grocery store. But that doesn't mean no one else has ever been there before.

In the eighteenth and early nineteenth centuries, "the West" was a vast wilderness that extended from the Mississippi River to the Pacific Ocean. The eleven explorers introduced in the following pages headed west without road maps, without highway signs, without any convenience stores along the way.

They knew the dangers, but faced them without hesitation. They left their homes, their friends, their families, the security of a roof over their heads and regular meals. They encountered wild animals. Some were attacked by Native Americans. Others were aided by the native peoples. Many nearly starved. All suffered under extreme weather conditions. Only five survived to old age. Most died young.

The explorers in this book were not the first people to see their discoveries. Native Americans had been living in North America for more than fourteen thousand years. But these men were the first people of European descent to gather the knowledge and bring information back to share with all mankind.

These eleven men came from different backgrounds. They lived in different time periods. And they were motivated to go west for various reasons. Most did not become famous. Only a few actually set records.

Yet each was uniquely qualified for his explorations. Each approached his journey with courage, enthusiasm, and confidence.

Each achieved amazing feats. And each, in turn, shared a common destiny: to learn more about that intriguing place called the American West.

NOTE TO THE READER

~✦══◉═══✦~

Explorers of the West. That's what this book is about.

This book focuses on the achievements of eleven lesser-known explorers. In fairness to these extraordinary individuals who survived some breathtaking situations, and out of respect to their memory, this book is, I hope, the story they would want told.

In an attempt to present the courageous and daring adventures of these eleven men as the eighteenth- and nineteenth-century white men that they were, a balanced account of many of the incidents is lacking. I fully acknowledge that these pages often do not represent the perspectives of the native peoples, or even of other white men. This in no way implies approval of all the explorers' actions, nor denial that other stories should be told.

I encourage the reader to seek more information. Other authors represent Native American experiences and opinions, and those works should be sought out. An excellent resource is a school or public library.

It is my hope that these pages will be just the beginning of a quest for more knowledge about the beautiful, amazing West.

—Charlotte Foltz Jones

"There are many voices from the past, and none should be silenced."
—Robin Fisher, *Vancouver's Voyage:*
Charting the Northwest Coast, 1791–1795

CHAPTER 1
Searching for a Northwest Passage

When Christopher Columbus left Spain in 1492, he was headed for the East Indies to trade for valuable spices. Columbus did not realize that North America would be in his way.

As soon as Europeans realized Columbus had actually bumped into a continent, explorers began searching for a shortcut around it or through it. Adventurers were interested in the riches of the Far East, rather than some unknown wilderness.

Waterways were essentially the superhighways in those years. Traveling overland was slow, difficult, and dangerous. A large river or water passage through the continent would mean a quicker, safer, easier way to get from the Atlantic Ocean to the Pacific Ocean.

Soon rumors, theories, and speculation circulated about a shortcut—commonly called the Northwest Passage. Many explorers searched the eastern seaboard of North America for this shortcut. The British parliament offered a reward to any British subject who could locate it.

In the late 1700s, trade for sea otter skins began between Europeans and the indigenous tribes living on North America's northwest coast. Trading ships sailed around Cape Horn in South America, then north to the coast of North America. As the ships sailed along the coast, they also searched for the western mouth of the fabled Northwest Passage.

In August 1775, Bruno Heceta, commander on the Spanish ship *Santiago*, sailed into a large bay that he named Bahiá de Asunción (Assumption Bay). Heceta believed it was the mouth of a great river and thought perhaps it was the

Jacques Cartier explored the
Gulf of St. Lawrence and
the St. Lawrence River in 1534
and 1535, but didn't find the
Northwest Passage.

waterway across the continent. Unfortunately, the current was so strong that Heceta couldn't get over the sandbar, but he recorded *Entrada* (meaning "entrance") on Spanish maps.

By 1788 John Meares, an English sea captain, had also found the opening to Heceta's great river. He could not get over the sandbar either, so he decided there was no river. He named it Deception Bay. Today it is called Bakers Bay. Meares named the northern cape Cape Disappointment, and that name is still used today.

In April 1792, another English captain named George Vancouver observed Heceta's *Entrada* from a distance. He agreed with Captain Meares's conclusion that there was no river.

It took the American seaman Captain Robert Gray to cross the sandbar and prove the river's existence. Gray named it Columbia's River.

The three men in this chapter influenced the development of the continent's Northwest in diverse ways, and each viewed the native people living in the region with very different attitudes.

While the Northwest Passage through the continent turned out to be a myth, the region as a whole held amazing surprises.

This picture, entitled *The Last Voyage of Henry Hudson*, is an artist's conception of the English explorer who died in 1611 on his fourth unsuccessful voyage to search for the Northwest Passage.

EXPEDITIONS OF GRAY, VANCOUVER, AND MACKENZIE (1787–1794)

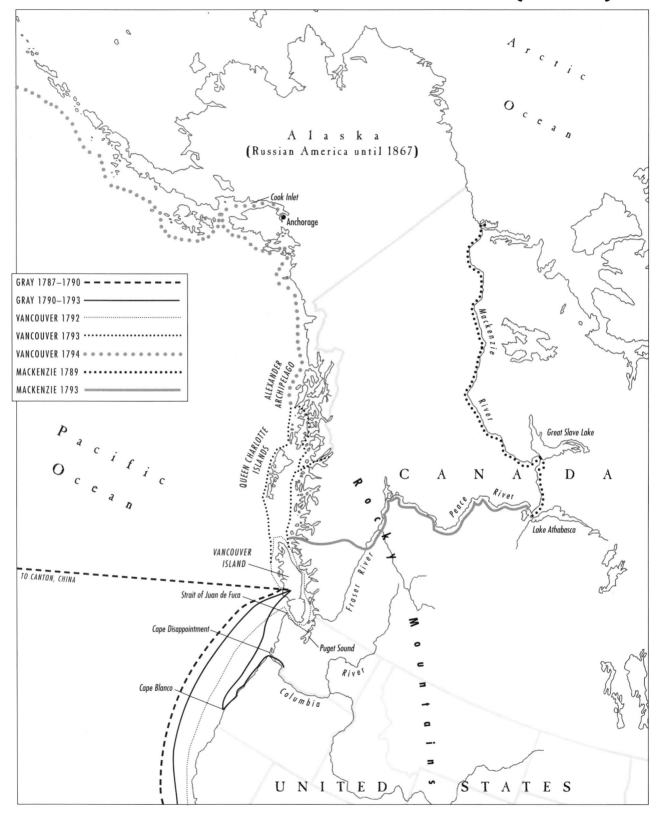

GRAY 1787–1790
GRAY 1790–1793
VANCOUVER 1792
VANCOUVER 1793
VANCOUVER 1794
MACKENZIE 1789
MACKENZIE 1793

Arctic Ocean

Alaska
(Russian America until 1867)

Cook Inlet
Anchorage

Mackenzie River

Great Slave Lake

Pacific Ocean

ALEXANDER ARCHIPELAGO

QUEEN CHARLOTTE ISLANDS

C A N A D A

Peace River

Lake Athabasca

R o c k y

VANCOUVER ISLAND

TO CANTON, CHINA

Strait of Juan de Fuca

Cape Disappointment

Fraser River

M o u n t a i n s

Puget Sound

Cape Blanco

River

Columbia

U N I T E D   S T A T E S

ROBERT GRAY (1755-1806)

American Ship Captain, Trader, Discoverer of the Columbia River,
First American Ship Captain to Circumnavigate the World

On May 12, 1792, Captain Robert Gray sailed the 212-ton ship *Columbia Redi-viva* across a sandbar in Deception Bay and into the body of water that would become the Columbia River. That 88-foot ship must have been an unbelievable spectacle to the Chinook people living beside the river.

The Chinooks' lives were changed forever that day, but one young man was probably more amazed than anyone else in the tribe. Twenty-seven-year-old Comcomly must have marveled at the captain of this awesome ship, since he was exactly like him in one important way: Captain Robert Gray and Comcomly each had only one eye. Imagine such a coincidence!

They couldn't know that day, but Comcomly would soon be chief of his Chinook tribe and would welcome the Lewis and Clark Expedition. The powerful Captain Robert Gray would sail away into obscurity.

Sometimes the least remarkable people have a most remarkable influence on history. Because Robert Gray seemed quite unremarkable, little is known about

It is believed this image of Captain Robert Gray was created after his death. Gray had only one eye, a fact the artist failed to illustrate.

him. He was born May 10, 1755, in Tiverton, Rhode Island. He was a mariner during the American Revolution, but it is not known whether he was in the navy or if he served aboard privately owned ships.

First Expedition: 1787–1790

In 1787, a Boston businessman named Joseph Barrell and five partners purchased two ships, hoping to make money on the sea otter fur trade on the northwest coast of North America. They appointed forty-seven-year-old John Kendrick as captain of the *Columbia Rediviva* (*Rediviva* is a Latin word meaning "reborn" or "restored to life") and commander of the expedition. Thirty-two-year-old Robert Gray, second in command, was in charge of a smaller ship, the sloop *Lady Washington*.

The *Columbia* and the *Lady Washington* were to sail south around Cape Horn in South America, then north to the west coast of North America. They carried trinkets—such as snuffboxes, rattraps, necklaces, earrings, Jew's harps, beads, commemorative medals, looking glasses, iron tools, and cooking utensils—in hopes of trading with the Native Americans for sea otter furs. The ships would then take the furs across the Pacific to China, trade for goods such as tea and silk, and return to Boston. The business partners had invested forty-nine thousand dollars in the venture and expected to make a profit reselling the Chinese goods in Boston.

The *Columbia*, with a crew of forty, and the *Lady Washington*, with a crew of ten, left Boston on September 30, 1787.

During the first part of the journey, Gray often disagreed with Kendrick's policies. On April 1, 1788, the *Columbia* and the *Lady Washington* were separated in a severe storm off Cape Horn. Gray considered the separation good luck. He sailed north, and on August 14, he dropped anchor in a bay on what is today's Oregon coast. He and his crew, most of whom were suffering from scurvy, were the first known non–Native Americans in Oregon.

Native Americans swarmed the ship, bringing berries and boiled crabs and furs to trade. Two days later, relations soured. A Native American stole a cutlass from a crew member on shore. A dispute erupted and the Native Americans

In this painting, Captain Robert Gray greets the Chinook people.

killed the crewman. The next morning, the *Lady Washington* left. The crew called the spot Murderers Harbour, but today it is called Tillamook Bay.

The *Lady Washington* sailed on to Nootka Sound, on present-day Vancouver Island, where Gray was to meet Captain Kendrick. When Gray arrived on September 16, two English ships were anchored in Friendly Cove and had already been trading for furs with the native peoples. A third vessel had been built there and was ready to launch.

The *Columbia* arrived a week later, after a harrowing journey in heavy storms. Most of Captain Kendrick's crew were suffering from scurvy, and two had died of the disease.

That fall the English ships sailed to the Sandwich Islands, today's Hawaiian Islands, to spend the winter, while the *Columbia* and the *Lady Washington* remained in Friendly Cove. By mid-March 1789, Gray was impatient to begin trading. He took the *Lady Washington* south and traded for sea otter pelts. When he returned six weeks later, he was annoyed that Kendrick had sailed the *Columbia* only four miles and still had not begun trading. In fact, Kendrick had made no effort to prepare the *Columbia* for the open seas.

When the *Lady Washington* arrived at Friendly Cove in Nootka Sound in 1788, Captain Gray was surprised to see British ships at anchor there. This illustration of a ship the British had built called the *North West America*, is from the journal of Captain John Meares. The *North West America* (on the right) is ready to be launched.

On May 2 Gray left again to trade, this time going north. Three weeks later, a storm battered the *Lady Washington* in the vicinity of today's Bucareli Bay in Alaska. The wind, rain, and high seas slammed the vessel against the rocks. Using lines, the crew worked frantically for two hours before they freed the ship and got her into open water.

The *Lady Washington* was badly damaged, so Gray headed back to Nootka Sound for repairs. When they arrived on June 17, the *Columbia* had not moved and Captain Kendrick still had not done any trading. Gray was probably exasperated, but he had no authority over Kendrick.

After the carpenters and blacksmiths repaired the *Lady Washington*, Kendrick suddenly and unexpectedly decided the two captains should switch vessels. Gray, as captain of the *Columbia*, would take the furs he had accumulated to China. Kendrick, as the new captain of the *Lady Washington*, planned to trade for furs along the coast.

Gray left Nootka on July 30. He stopped to resupply in the Sandwich Islands. While anchored there, a young Hawaiian named Attoo joined the crew.

Gray arrived in China in November 1789. He sold his furs, purchased 21,462 pounds of bohea tea, and left the Orient in late January 1790. The *Columbia* sailed around the Cape of Good Hope at the southern tip of Africa and arrived in Boston on August 10, 1790. The trip had taken 2 years, 314 days.

Gray was the first American sea captain to sail through the treacherous waters around Cape Horn, *and* he went through the passage in the worst of winter weather. He was the first known American to command a ship that visited the northwest coast of North America, and the *Columbia* was the first American ship to visit the Sandwich Islands. The *Columbia* had sailed almost forty-two thousand miles and was the first American ship to carry the United States flag completely around the world.

On the *Columbia*'s arrival in Boston, people gathered on the wharfs to welcome the ship. Most of Boston's eighteen thousand residents cheered as the crew paraded up State Street. Walking with Gray at the head of the parade was Attoo, the Sandwich Island boy. Attoo wore a cloak and helmet made entirely of scarlet and gold bird feathers from his native island.

Unfortunately, by the time the *Columbia* arrived in Boston, much of the tea had been damaged by the salty ocean water that leaked into the ship's cargo hold. Barrell and his partners lost money on the venture.

Nevertheless, Barrell sponsored a second voyage.

Second Expedition: 1790–1793

Gray remained in Boston about seven weeks. As captain of the *Columbia Rediviva,* he took six thousand dollars' worth of trade goods and left Boston on September 28, 1790 for a second trip to the American Northwest.

The *Columbia* arrived at Vancouver Island the first week of June 1791. The trip had taken almost four months less than it had with Kendrick in command. However, ten men were suffering from scurvy. They were taken ashore, buried in

Columbia *in Destress* [sic] was made by George Davidson, the *Columbia*'s painter, after the ship had rounded Cape Horn on its second voyage to the northwest coast and was severley damaged in a storm on December 11, 1790.

earth up to their hips, and given "greens" to eat. All of the men recovered, probably because of the "greens."

Between the time Gray left the Northwest Coast in July 1789 and the time he returned, Kendrick told Gray he had "sold" himself the sloop *Lady Washington*. In a letter to Joseph Barrell, Kendrick called it a "sham sale" and said it was "merely to help me through my difficulties and troubles."

Who really owned the *Lady Washington*? No one is sure. Even historians are confused! Kendrick continued to command the *Lady Washington*, and he went into the fur trading business for himself. He never sent payment to the owners back in Boston. Kendrick was killed in 1794 in the Sandwich Islands.

Gray traded up and down the coast during the summer of 1791, but he was always cautious when dealing with the Native Americans. People from most of the tribes carried bows and arrows, spears, or daggers and committed petty thievery.

On August 12, Gray anchored the *Columbia* in a cove off Clarence Strait in today's Alaska. Early that morning, three crewmen went fishing. A few hours later, Captain Gray wanted to get under way in order to take advantage of the wind. The ship fired cannon shots as a signal for the men to return.

Receiving no response, a search crew left, but soon returned with flag at half-mast. Native peoples had killed the three seamen and stolen their clothes and weapons. The crew buried their friends and called the place Massacre Cove. Today it is known as Port Tempest.

During the fall of 1791, Gray's men built a small fort on Vancouver Island, which they named Fort Defiance. That winter, the *Columbia's* crew and the Nootkan people exchanged many acts of friendship. The crew shared their Christmas dinner with the Nootkans, and Captain Gray went to the Nootkan village Opisat when one of the chiefs was ill. He even allowed the chief to sleep on board the *Columbia.*

Over the winter, the crew built another sloop with which to do trading. It was the first American vessel built on the northwest coast. Named the *Adventure,* it was launched February 23, 1792.

Meanwhile, the villagers grew tired of the visitors and began preparing their weapons for war. Attoo, the cabin boy, admitted to Captain Gray that one of the

Winter Quarters illustrates Fort Defiance. The painter, *Columbia* crew member George Davidson, is pictured on the right showing another crewman his illustration (this picture!). The sloop *Adventure*, built by the *Columbia* crew, is shown on shore near the building.

chiefs had offered to make him a great chief if he would help kill the ship's crew that night.

Gray divided his men between the fort and the ship. In the middle of the night, the Nootkans began whooping and shrieking. When they realized the ship's crew was ready for the attack, they retreated. The incident angered Gray.

The *Columbia* and the *Adventure* left Fort Defiance at the end of March. Robert Haswell, who had been first mate on the *Columbia*, commanded the *Adventure* and took it north to trade, while Gray took the *Columbia* south to trade there. Before the *Columbia* left the area, Gray wanted revenge for the attempted massacre, and he ordered his crew to burn Opitsat, the Nootkan village.

The men followed Gray's orders, even though they did not want to burn the two hundred wooden buildings so beautifully decorated with native artwork. John Boit, fifth mate on the *Columbia,* wrote in his journal, "This fine village, the work of Ages, was in a short time totally destroy'd." The village had been the largest in the Northwest.

There is another side to the story. The Nootkans denied that they had attempted a massacre and later said that they had refused to trade with Gray and insisted that was why he burned their village.

By April 11, the *Columbia* got as far south as Cape Blanco on the southern coast of Oregon, and then headed north again. During the last week of April, the *Columbia* encountered two English ships off the coast of today's Washington State. The *Discovery* and the *Chatham* were commanded by Captain George Vancouver.

Lieutenant Peter Puget and surgeon-naturalist Archibald Menzies boarded the *Columbia,* representing Vancouver. They told Gray their ships were on a "voyage of discovery" to search for the Northwest Passage. Their destination was the Strait of Juan de Fuca. Gray shared his knowledge of the area.

After the ships parted, the *Columbia* went south and entered a harbor that is now known as Gray's Harbor. While they were anchored, the Chinook came to trade. On the afternoon of May 10, Gray left the harbor and sailed all night. It is believed he had received some information from the Chinook about the existence of a great river.

On May 11, 1792, Captain Robert Gray made his most famous discovery, a previously unexplored river. He named it after his ship, and today it is still known as the Columbia River.

Gray, who sailed his ship twenty-five miles up the river, was the first white man to explore it. His discovery, and the fact that he sailed up the river, gave the United States claim to Oregon in later land disputes.

The *Columbia* spent almost two weeks in the estuary, trading with the Chinook. Then Gray sailed over the sandbar and back into the Pacific Ocean on May 20.

During the last week of June, a storm slammed the *Columbia* against a ridge of rocks, severely damaging it. Gray returned to Friendly Cove, which was now ruled by the Spanish. The Spanish governor, Don Francisco de la Bodega y Quadra, provided Gray with hospitality and assistance.

In early June 1792, Native Americans (probably Kwakiutl) attacked the *Columbia*
off the southern end of Vancouver Island. This image of the event
was made by George Davidson, the ship's painter.

While the ship was being repaired, Governor Bodega y Quadra invited officers of the British and American ships to dine with the Spanish officers. John
Boit was amazed and described the July 29 event: "[F]ifty four persons sat down
to dinner, and the plates, which was solid silver, was shifted 5 times, which made
270 plates."

Before leaving the northwest coast, Gray told Governor Bodega y Quadra
about entering the Columbia River, and shared the map he had drawn. Gray also
sold him the sloop *Adventure*.

The *Columbia* left the northwest coast for the Far East on October 3, 1792.
In China, Gray traded his furs for tea, nankeens (handwoven cotton fabric), sugar,

and Chinese porcelain. He left China and sailed around the Cape of Good Hope, arriving in Boston Harbor on July 20, 1793. The trip had taken 2 years, 295 days.

The goal of Gray's voyages was to make a profit for his employers. He was often cruel and ruthless in his dealings with the native peoples and was sometimes harsh with his own crewmen.

On his first journey, Gray had been the first American sea captain to go completely around the world in one journey. On his second voyage, Gray discovered, named, and claimed for the United States one of the continent's greatest rivers. These were formidible accomplishments.

But when Gray returned to Boston, he faded into obscurity. After 1793, he traded up and down the Atlantic coast and in England. He married Martha Atkins in 1794 and they had four children. Gray died of yellow fever in 1806 on a voyage to Charleston, South Carolina, and was buried at sea.

GEORGE VANCOUVER (1757-1798)
British Navy Captain, Diplomat, Explorer,
Surveyor of the Northwest Coast and Sandwich Islands

At the age of sixteen, George Vancouver was an "Able-Bodied Midshipman" serving under the famous Captain James Cook on the English ship *Resolution*. On January 30, 1774, the *Resolution* was in the Antarctic Regions and had sailed farther south than any other vessel. Stopped by hundred-foot mountains of ice, the 426-ton ship was about to turn back when Vancouver climbed to the end of the bowsprit. Hanging off the front of the ship, he waved his hat in the air and announced, *"Ne plus ultra"* (Latin for "not more beyond"). By this he meant, "I am nearer the South Pole than any other man!"

It was true. For years he could claim to have been closer to the South Pole than any other person.

George Vancouver, the youngest of six children, was born June 22, 1757, in King's

This is the only portrait of Captain George Vancouver that has ever been identified. Here, only a detail of the painting is shown. Recently scholars have begun to doubt that this image actually is George Vancouver.

Lynn, Norfolk, England. His mother died when he was eleven years old, and he entered the Royal Navy when he was fourteen.

It was common for ships' captains to choose boys to go to sea, and Captain James Cook selected Vancouver to join his second voyage of exploration. When the *Resolution* set sail on July 13, 1772, Vancouver had just turned fifteen.

During the journey, he received instruction in seamanship, nautical astronomy, observing, surveying, and drawing maps. Cook was known as the world's greatest sea surveyor, so Vancouver had the world's best instructor. The boys serving on Cook's ship also learned the skills of sailors: how to hand and reef the sails, steer the ship, and fire small arms.

After the voyage Vancouver was promoted to midshipman and sailed on Cook's third voyage.

By 1788, English ships were on the northwest coast of North America, trading with the Native Americans for furs. When a dispute erupted between the

Spanish and the British at Nootka Sound, Vancouver was assigned to reclaim the British property. He was also to survey the Sandwich Islands and the northwest coast of North America, and to search for the Northwest Passage.

Vancouver commanded the 331-ton ship *Discovery* with one hundred men aboard. Accompanying the *Discovery* was the 131-ton *Chatham*, with forty-five men aboard, commanded by Lieutenant William R. Broughton.

Vancouver left Falmouth, England, on April 1, 1791. He charted and mapped parts of Australia, New Zealand, Tahiti, and the Sandwich Islands, where he delighted and astonished the natives with a fireworks display.

First Expedition: 1792

Vancouver reached the California coast on April 18, 1792. He then sailed north, and by April 27, he reached Cape Disappointment. Vancouver noticed an inlet, but it did not appear accessible to his large ships. He dismissed the "river coloured water" as "streams falling into the bay." With this decision, Vancouver missed discovering what Captain Robert Gray would name Columbia's River two weeks later.

But Vancouver's orders were to search for a Northwest Passage—a waterway suitable for oceangoing vessels to travel through the continent. Since large ships could not navigate on rivers, he did not intend to explore them. Besides, it was believed the Northwest Passage was farther north, possibly through the Strait of Juan de Fuca.

Two days later Vancouver spotted the first foreign sailing vessel he had seen in eight months. It was Captain Gray in the *Columbia*.

Lieutenant Peter Puget and Archibald Menzies met with Gray aboard the *Columbia*. They exchanged information about the Strait of Juan de Fuca and the mouth of a river, which both ships had been unable to enter.

After the meeting, Vancouver continued north to begin surveying. The large ships could not maneuver in the inlets and narrow straits, so the mapping parties used small boats.

The surveying was a slow process, but day by day the men mapped the inlets, bays, canals, and channels. They sketched the shorelines and prominent land features, measured angles between headlands with the sextant, took compass bearings, made longitude and lunar observations, and checked their observations with their chronometers. At noon each day, they used the sun to establish their latitude. But the fog and clouds common on the northwest coast often hid the sun, making the job more difficult.

Lieutenant Puget and Joseph Whidbey were on a surveying expedition in May when they encountered a canoe full of Native Americans. Puget floated

This drawing by John Sykes, a member of Captain Vancouver's expedition, shows the small surveying boats in Admiralty Inlet in 1792, with Mount Rainier in the background.

John Sykes made this sketch of Lieutenant Puget's camp, which the men set up
while surveying in what is now called Puget Sound.

some trinkets to them. They came nearer but responded to questions with "Poo
Poo." One crew member interpreted this as their imitation of the sound of
gunfire.

Suddenly the Native Americans drew their weapons and threatened an attack.
Puget ordered the men to fire the swivel gun. Grapeshot scattered over the water,
and the Native Americans withdrew.

When Puget's party returned to the main ship after eight days, they had
traced the upper part of a sound. Vancouver named it Puget Sound in honor of
his lieutenant.

Near the middle of June, Vancouver missed finding another great river
known as the Fraser.

Late in the afternoon of August 6, the *Discovery* ran into a submerged reef.
Small boats from the *Chatham* rushed to help, but the tide receded before they

Discovery *on the Rocks* shows the Haida natives watching as Vancouver's ship *Discovery* runs aground on a reef on August 6, 1792. The *Chatham* is shown in the background of this picture by Zachary Mudge, a member of Vancouver's expedition.

could free the ship. Sitting high on the rocks, the *Discovery* leaned dangerously to the side, threatening to keel over. Vancouver wrote that the "situation ... was alarming in the highest degree." Five hours later the tide reached its lowest ebb, and the crew could only hope that the *Discovery* would not capsize.

Early the next morning, the tide came in and the *Discovery* again floated upright. Amazingly, it was not damaged.

The next afternoon the *Chatham* was stranded among rocks when the tide receded. When the tide came back in the next morning, the *Chatham* also floated free with no serious damage.

Over the summer Vancouver's crew surveyed through Queen Charlotte Sound and the *Discovery* became the first ship to completely circumnavigate Vancouver Island. This was a real feat, since the waterway between the island and the mainland remains treacherous to this day.

Vancouver's assignment included taking possession of the Spanish settlement in Nootka Sound. When Vancouver met Governor Bodega y Quadra on August 19, they quickly became friends. The governor was extremely gracious and provided a daily treat of hot rolls, fresh milk, and vegetables. He also served the *Discovery's* officers a five-course dinner. They had not eaten so well since they left England. Bodega y Quadra told Vancouver about the river Captain Gray had entered and named Columbia's River. He also gave Vancouver the sketch Gray had made of it.

Vancouver and Bodega y Quadra could not agree on the details for the property transfer. Because of their friendship, they decided to let their governments back in Europe resolve the matter. They commemorated their friendship by

This drawing, *A View of Friendly Cove in Nootka Sound,* is by Harry Humphrys, a member of Vancouver's expedition. It illustrates how the area looked when Captain Vancouver and Spanish Governor Bodega y Quadra met. Nootka Sound is now a part of British Columbia, Canada.

This picture is a contemporary version of the ships of Vancouver and
Bodega y Quadra at anchor in Friendly Cove.

naming the island Quadra and Vancouver Island, but today it is known as Vancouver Island in British Columbia.

Vancouver left Nootka Sound in the fall of 1792, and on October 19, his ships approached the mouth of Columbia's River. The *Discovery* could not get over the sandbar, but the *Chatham* made it through. Its small boats sailed up the river and reached the site of today's Vancouver, Washington State, and Portland, Oregon.

The *Discovery* and the *Chatham* spent the 1792–1793 winter surveying the Sandwich Islands. On Hawaii Island Chief Keeaumoku wanted to buy firearms to fight the people on neighboring islands. Vancouver refused, saying that killing one another would be destructive. Instead, he gave them cattle and sheep. He explained that as the livestock multiplied, the large herds would mean greater wealth, which would mean even greater power. Vancouver is credited for today's cattle industry in the Hawaiian Islands.

Second Expedition: 1793

In April 1793, Vancouver returned to the northwest coast. He arrived at the Bella Coola inlet on June 4, and missed meeting the explorer Alexander Mackenzie by only seven weeks.

Over the summer of 1793, Vancouver surveyed the fjords, channels, and waters of northern British Columbia, Alaska's Inside Passage, and Queen Charlotte Sound. During one twenty-three-day period, the small boats rowed seven hundred miles in and out of inlets. Yet they only moved north sixty miles.

On August 12, at Revillagigedo Island in today's southern Alaska, several Tlingit canoes approached, appearing peaceful. Then they suddenly became noisy and an old lady started screaming orders. Vancouver described her as a "vixen" with "a remarkably large lip ornament." The Tlingit grabbed everything they could from the boats, including firearms. Vancouver tried to negotiate, and finally both sides laid down their arms.

The crisis seemed to be over. Then the old woman again yelled orders, and the Tlingit resumed their attack. Since Vancouver had so few men and there were so many Native Americans, he ordered his men to fire. Six to ten Tlingit were killed, and two of Vancouver's men were injured. Vancouver named the site Escape Point, and that name is still used today.

During that summer, Vancouver was unwell and often stayed in his cabin. The following October, the ships sailed to the Sandwich Islands, where Vancouver continued the surveying work.

Third Expedition: 1794

In March 1794 Vancouver sailed to the southern coast of Alaska and Cook Inlet, which is today's Anchorage, Alaska. Sleet and ice storms were terrible. The *Discovery*'s thermometer read twenty-five degrees. Ice floated on the water. But Vancouver's crew completed surveying Cook Inlet by the first week of May.

Many of the men aboard the *Discovery* and the *Chatham* were ill, including Vancouver. Despite their poor health, the crew continued surveying and finally finished on August 19, 1794. They named the last site Port Conclusion. The men aboard both ships celebrated, gave "three exulting cheers," and exchanged congratulations. Vancouver gave his men "an additional allowance of grog as was fully sufficient to answer every purpose of festivity on the occasion."

The ships left Port Conclusion on August 22 and returned to England, arriving October 16, 1795. Vancouver had been promoted to captain.

Vancouver was a perfectionist. Although the geography of the northwest coast of North America is extremely complicated, his maps were remarkably accurate and were used by sea captains for most of the nineteenth century. The 1791–1795 voyage was the longest surveying expedition up to that time. The *Discovery* was gone for 4 years, 8 months, and 29 days. The expedition sailed 65,000 miles. But in order to explore every inlet and cove, it is estimated that the small boats rowed 10,000 miles.

Vancouver's relations with the Native American people were those of an interested observer, and there were few serious clashes, probably because he insisted on fairness. Peter Puget wrote in his journal that their barter with the Native Americans was "carried on with the Strictest Honesty on both Sides . . . we would never accept any Article till the owner was satisfied with what was offered in Exchange."

As a ship's captain, Vancouver commanded with strict military discipline. The scurvy occurrence, number of accidents, and death rate among Vancouver's crew were very low. Vancouver ordered more floggings than average captains. Floggings were standard discipline for seamen but not for midshipmen, who were considered officers. However, in 1794 Vancouver disciplined Midshipman Thomas Pitt with a flogging, and then discharged him. He sent Pitt and two others home on a supply ship.

Pitt's father had recently died, and the nineteen-year-old midshipman had acquired the title of the Second Baron Camelford while at sea. Young Baron Camelford wanted revenge for the floggings and for his dismissal from the *Discovery*. In September 1796, he challenged Vancouver to a duel. Vancouver offered to let a navy officer judge the case. Instead, Baron Camelford attacked Vancouver and his brother, creating a public scandal. In those times, many British placed less value on a person's accomplishments and more value on his family and ranking in the royal hierarchy. For that reason, this incident with the Second Baron Camelford ruined Vancouver's reputation.

George Vancouver died on May 12, 1798. He had never married and left no direct descendants.

ALEXANDER MACKENZIE (1764-1820)

*Explorer, Canadian Fur Trader, First White Man to Descend the
Mackenzie River to the Arctic Ocean, First White Man to
Cross the North American Continent North of Mexico*

Alexander Mackenzie was twenty-nine years old when he became the first person to cross the North American continent north of Mexico. Pleased with his accomplishment, he took time out to paint his name on a rock near the Pacific Ocean. Using vermillion mixed with grease, he wrote: "Alexander Mackenzie, from Canada by land, the twenty-second of July, one thousand seven hundred and ninety-three."

As Mackenzie painted, hostile Bella Bella tribesmen threatened to attack his party. Terrified, his men asked Mackenzie if he planned to remain there so that they would all be killed. The men were lucky to escape with their lives.

*   *   *

This portrait of Mackenzie was painted by Sir Thomas Lawrence around 1800.

Alexander Mackenzie was born in 1764 in Scotland, the third of four children. His mother died before he was eleven. Alexander sailed to New York with his father and two aunts in 1775. Three years later, he was sent to Montreal to attend school.

The next year he went to work as a clerk for a fur trade company, Finlay and Gregory and Company. After five years he was made a partner, and in 1787 Mackenzie was assigned to Fort Liard in present-day Alberta, Canada. At Fort Liard, the British traded for beaver pelts with the Native Americans.

Peter Pond, the trader in charge of the post, changed Mackenzie's life over the 1787–1788 winter. Pond believed a river flowed from Great Slave Lake to the Pacific Ocean. Mackenzie studied Pond's hand-drawn maps, which indicated that the Pacific Ocean was not far away. Mackenzie became obsessed with finding the river and finding a route to the Pacific.

As it turned out, Pond's maps were seven hundred miles off course, and the river flowing to the Pacific Ocean did not exist.

First Expedition: 1789

Though he was a small man, Alexander Mackenzie was a determined, ambitious, strong, and demanding leader. Surprisingly, he was generally patient with the Native American people he encountered.

On June 3, 1789, Mackenzie left Fort Chipewyan, in present-day Alberta, Canada, and headed for the Pacific Ocean. With him were four French Canadian voyageurs, two of their wives, a young German, and six Chipewyan guides, including one known as the English Chief. Traveling in four canoes, they took the Slave River.

Two days later, one of the canoes wrecked in the rapids, and they lost all the supplies packed in that canoe. They reached a frozen Great Slave Lake on June 9. The cold and stormy weather forced them to camp for six days. Despite the frigid temperatures, they were tormented by mosquitoes.

On June 15, they set out again, but rains, high winds, and freezing temperatures plagued them as they negotiated their way through the broken ice on the lake. Even their Chipewyan guides got lost in the fog and the maze of bays, rocks, and trees.

Finally, on June 29, they located the headwaters of the river that Pond had shown on his map. The river's current was swift and strong, making it difficult to navigate. They were in the "Land of the Midnight Sun," and Mackenzie pushed his people to start paddling the canoes as early as 3 A.M. and continue until nine at night.

Ice was piled high on the riverbanks, and now flies tormented them. But the river went west—just as Peter Pond's maps had showed.

Then, on July 2, they sighted a chain of mountains in front of them. Since rivers can't flow uphill to cross mountains, they knew the river must change

As shown in the above 1825 illustration, Mackenzie's west-flowing river
soon faced a ridge of mountains. When Mackenzie saw the mountains in front of him,
he realized the river would not flow to the Pacific Ocean.

course and flow north. Mackenzie realized Pond's maps were wrong, and the river would *not* lead to the Pacific Ocean.

Local Slave and Dogrib people advised Mackenzie not to continue. They warned of rapids, waterfalls, and horrible monsters. Mackenzie ignored the warnings and pushed on.

On July 12, Mackenzie's party reached the mouth of the river. But they had not reached the Pacific Ocean. They had reached the Arctic Ocean, which Mackenzie called the Hyperborean Sea. He referred to the river as Grand River or the River Disappointment. The party spent four nights on a treeless island, which Mackenzie named Whale Island. Today it is called Garry Island. They began their return journey on July 16.

It had taken them six weeks to reach the sea, but their return trip took eight weeks because they were paddling against the river's current. When they arrived at Fort Chipewyan on September 12, they had traveled 3,000 miles in 102 days.

Mackenzie was the first white man to follow one of North America's greatest rivers all the way to the Arctic Ocean. It was later named the Mackenzie River in his honor. Despite his amazing accomplishment, Mackenzie was disappointed. Fur traders needed a river flowing west to the Pacific Ocean. He couldn't see any practical use for a river flowing to the frozen north.

Unfortunately, Mackenzie was not a surveyor and he had neither the proper training nor the necessary instruments to take precise readings of his locations. For that reason his maps were not accurate. So Mackenzie spent the following year in London, studying geography, astronomy, surveying, navigating by the stars, and using a sextant. He also bought some instruments—a compass, sextant, chronometer, and telescope.

Mackenzie was determined to try again to reach the Pacific Ocean. In 1792, he returned to Fort Chipewyan and then traveled by canoe to the fork of the Peace and Smoky rivers. His men built a fort, which they named Fort Fork, in today's Alberta, Canada.

Over the winter, Mackenzie's men built a special twenty-five-foot canoe that was extremely strong, yet light. Meanwhile, Mackenzie learned all he could from the Native Americans in the area. He valued their knowledge and wrote in

This illustration by Frederic Remington shows one of the Native American guides offering Mackenzie advice.

a letter to his cousin Roderic, "[W]ithout Indians I have very little hopes of succeeding."

Second Expedition: 1793

On May 9, 1793, Mackenzie left Fort Fork, again heading for the Pacific Ocean. With him were Alexander MacKay, clerk and second in command; six French Canadian voyageurs; and two young Beaver men to serve as interpreters and hunters. Two of the voyageurs had accompanied Mackenzie on his first expedition.

The canoe was packed with three thousand pounds of supplies, equipment, scientific instruments, provisions, gifts for the Native Americans, arms, and ammunition. A dog also went along, which they referred to as "our dog."

Mackenzie's two expeditions were made in a canoe similar to this one, which is about to descend over a rapid. This painting, called *Running a Rapid*, is by Frances Anne Hopkins.

They traveled west on the Peace River, but the next day the canoe began to leak. They landed, unloaded it, and used a sticky plant gum to repair the first of many leaks.

The men paddled upstream, but in many places the strong river current made it necessary to pole the canoe. Sometimes they used ropes and pulled the canoe up through rapids.

They often carried their gear around the rapids. The men repeated this process, called portaging, again and again. In one two-mile stretch, they portaged four times. The steep, slippery riverbank and the thick, tangled growth made carrying their three thousand pounds of gear an exhausting job.

By May 21 the river had become completely impassable. The men cut a trail and carried their gear and the canoe overland. The seven-mile detour took them three days.

Back on the river, the deafening roar of the water made it almost impossible for the men to hear Mackenzie's orders. Worse, gigantic rocks rolled down the mountainsides, often narrowly missing them.

In Peace River Canyon, steep, overhanging cliffs enclosed rocky cascades and rapids. In one place, vertical rock canyon walls forced the men to paddle and pole the canoe up the treacherous rapids, since there was no way to portage around.

The men were exhausted and wanted to turn back, but Mackenzie would not even consider the idea. The only one not exhausted was "our dog." He happily performed his duties and on May 30 barked an alarm when a wolf paraded on a nearby ridge.

This image is entitled *Canadian Voyageurs Walking a Canoe Up a Rapid.*
Sometimes the voyageurs could use poles to work their way up rapids or small waterfalls,
but often they had to wade in the ice-cold water to maneuver the canoe.

This illustration, *Indians Completing a Portage*, shows how difficult it was to portage.

At the headwaters of the Peace River in today's British Columbia, Mackenzie had to choose which fork to take. Today they are the Finlay and Parsnip rivers. An old man of the Beaver tribe had advised Mackenzie to take the more dangerous south fork, the Parsnip. It would lead to a carrying place, which was a day's march overland to a great river. Mackenzie followed the old man's advice, but almost immediately doubted his decision. The men struggled to keep the canoe moving in the strong current, and the mosquitoes nearly drove them crazy.

On June 9, they encountered a group of very poor Sekani people: three men, three women, and eight children. They had heard of white men, but were still terrified by the sight of the men. Mackenzie gave them food, beads, and other gifts. He gave the children bits of sugar, something they had never tasted before.

One of the Sekani men knew of a great river. He drew a map on a piece of bark and went along as a guide.

High in the mountains they came to a lake, now called Arctic Lake, where the party found some baskets other Native Americans had left hanging from tree limbs. Mackenzie helped himself to a net, some hooks, a goat's horn, and a wooden groundhog trap. In exchange he left a knife, some fire steels, beads, and awls.

The men carried their canoe and gear over a ridge now known as the Great Divide. Here the waters flow either west to the Pacific Ocean or east to the Atlantic Ocean. They were the first Europeans to cross the Continental Divide north of Spanish Mexico. From that point on, the men traveled with the river's current instead of against it. But banks of gravel and trees that had fallen across the river made navigating the waterway difficult.

To gain the goodwill and assistance of the Native Americans, the explorers carried gifts. Mackenzie often gave the children sugar, a treat they had never tasted before.

On the morning of June 13, the canoe hit a rock and crashed into a sandbar. As the men tried to straighten it, the current swept the canoe into deep water and then slammed it against a boulder. The steersman was thrown out of his seat, and another man was catapulted onto the riverbank, nearly killing him.

The canoe hurtled to the opposite shore, smashed into another rock, plunged through some rapids, and finally drifted into shallow water.

The Beaver and Sekani guides watched the catastrophe from the shore. They were so upset they sobbed and wept, but the rapids were so dangerous they could not even offer help.

Miraculously, no one had been killed, and there were no broken bones. All the party's gear, however, had been dumped into the fast-running river. With arms and legs numb from the ice-cold water, the men retrieved as many belongings as possible. The canoe was seriously damaged and most of their supplies had been lost, including their musket balls. Their gunpowder was soaked.

After this near disaster, the men informed Mackenzie they were returning home.

Mackenzie listened patiently. Then he said they should be thankful no one was injured. He reminded them that they knew of the possible dangers when they joined the expedition. He brought up the disgrace they would face from other voyageurs if they quit. He shamed them for losing their courage and stressed how he depended on their strength of character. He agreed the canoe was damaged but said he trusted them to make the necessary repairs.

By the time Mackenzie had finished talking, all agreed they would follow him wherever he led.

Two days later, they resumed their journey. With four men in the canoe, the others carried gear overland, cutting through the tangled mountain vegetation. Progress was agonizingly slow.

Finally they reached the "great river" the Sekani man knew about, the present-day McGregor, and it was much easier to navigate. But in the middle of the night, the Sekani guide disappeared.

They followed the McGregor for a short distance, then took another river known as the Fraser. Two days later they encountered a band of Native Americans who shot arrows at them, but no one was injured.

In this night-scene painting, *Canoe Party Around Campfire* by Frances Anne Hopkins, the voyageurs are patching their canoe with gum from trees. After patching and repatching, the gum substance made the canoe very heavy to carry.

A few miles farther, they encountered more hostile people. This time Mackenzie went ashore alone and faced them. He had pistols tucked in his belt—just in case! He gave the adults mirrors, beads, and knives, and he gave the children bits of sugar. These were Carriers, and they invited Mackenzie and his men into their camp.

They told Mackenzie that the river went south, not west. They warned of rapids, enormous waterfalls, cliffs, and canyons of towering rock walls. They also warned of tribes who would kill them. Mackenzie ignored the warnings and continued down the river. Two days later, he found the Carriers were right. On June 23 the expedition turned back.

This morning scene, *Voyageurs at Dawn* by Frances Anne Hopkins, shows the difficult living conditions of the voyageurs' camps. The adventurers slept on the hard ground every night, often in below-freezing temperatures, on expeditions that lasted for months.

By June 27, the men agreed that their canoe had been smashed and crashed too many times and that the gum substance used to make repairs had made the canoe too heavy to lift. The men began constructing a new canoe and finished it on July 1.

Three days later, the party prepared to go overland. They buried a cache of food and gunpowder, and hid their canoe and gear under large pieces of timber. Carrying packs, they hiked the steep coastal mountains. The wind blew and they were pelted with hail, snow, and rain. As they climbed higher and higher, the men nearly froze as they crossed a six-thousand-foot pass now known as Macken-zie Pass. Mackenzie wrote that "the weather was as distressing as any I had ever experienced."

The men were exhausted and had little to eat. They met many groups of people as they crossed the difficult terrain. Luckily, none was hostile. Macken-zie persuaded, bribed, and, in some cases, forced various men to serve as guides.

On July 16, a Carrier man and his wife joined them and made a kettle of fish roe (fish eggs) cooked in a terrible-smelling, rancid oil. The Carriers considered it a delicacy. Mackenzie was sickened by the smell, but his men were so hungry that they ate it anyway.

On the evening of July 17, they came down out of the mountains and into a Bella Coola village. The village chief and his people welcomed the men and served them roast salmon. Mackenzie named the settlement Friendly Village.

The next day it took only a few hours to get to a second, larger Bella Coola village. The chief hugged Mackenzie. His oldest son gave Mackenzie a robe made of sea otter—a very high honor. Then they served a three-hour feast.

Mackenzie called this Great Village. He gave the chief a pair of scissors as a gift. The chief was puzzled and didn't know what to do with them, so Mackenzie showed him how he could cut and trim his long beard. The chief was delighted.

The chief of Great Village loaned Mackenzie one of his canoes plus four people to paddle for the final stretch of the journey to the ocean. One of the four was the chief's son.

When Mackenzie was ready to leave, his ax was missing. He insisted the ax be returned. Finally, it was found under the chief's canoe. After all the hospitality, it was a very uncomfortable situation.

The men also could not find "our dog" and eventually left without him.

The next day they reached the Pacific Ocean in what is now known as Dean Channel. A group of Bella Bella men indicated that a large canoe carrying white men had been in the bay recently. They said a man named "Macubah" fired at them. Historians assume "Macubah" was their word for Vancouver. However, Vancouver's journals do not mention the incident.

The Bella Bella harassed Mackenzie's men, stole small items, and threatened to kill them. Mackenzie's men were probably scared, but Mackenzie had crossed the entire continent and was determined to make his scientific observations and record his findings as accurately as possible. Then, while his men waited impatiently, Mackenzie mixed some vermillion with grease and wrote his name on a rock.

When Mackenzie's party returned to Great Village on July 25, the chief was worried that his son might have been killed. Although the son was safe, the chief was still upset. Mackenzie gave him cloth, knives, and other gifts, then quickly left to avoid any kind of confrontation.

The men finally found "our dog," and the party retraced their route over the mountains. On August 4, they reached the river where they had cached their canoe and gear. Everything was in good condition.

Spirits were high as they traveled up the Fraser River. The men were happy to be back in their canoe. After they crossed the Great Divide, the current flowed downstream. On August 18, they covered in one day the distance it had taken them seven days to navigate going the other direction.

The weather warmed, and when they came through Peace River Canyon, they found plenty of game. They had not eaten well for weeks, so everyone was glad to feast.

The expedition arrived at Fort Fork on August 24, and the party joyously

Mackenzie wrote his name on this rock when he reached the Pacific Ocean. While his "grease and vermillion" letters washed away centuries ago, the words have been restored.

fired their guns and displayed their flag for the two men who had remained at the fort. They had been gone 108 days and traveled 2,400 miles (including 520 miles covered on foot). There were no deaths or serious injuries on the journey.

Although he had a few difficulties with some Native Americans, Mackenzie had used diplomacy and did not fire any shots in anger. Mackenzie was very controlling and had a temper, so his relationships with the Native Americans he met were often tense. But he listened to their advice and often relied on their knowledge to insure the safety and success of the expedition.

Considering his equipment, Mackenzie's survey readings were surprisingly accurate on his second expedition.

Mackenzie was the first European to cross the North American continent north of Mexico. Yet once he returned, people hardly took note of his accomplishments. He tried to convince his partners in the North West Company that they should extend their trading empire across the continent to the Pacific Ocean. But the partners were not interested in his ideas, and Mackenzie finally let his contract expire.

He moved to London in 1799 and established his own fur trading company. In 1801, he published a book about his voyages: *Voyages from Montreal, on the River St. Laurence, through the Continent of North America to the Frozen and Pacific Oceans, in the Years, 1789 and 1793.* England's King George III knighted Mackenzie in 1802.

Mackenzie returned to Canada, and from 1804 to 1808 he was a member of the House of Assembly of Lower Canada. He remained interested in the fur trade the rest of his life.

At least one important man read Mackenzie's book: Thomas Jefferson. Jefferson, the third president of the United States, realized the new nation must move west. When Meriwether Lewis and William Clark went on their expedition to the Pacific, they took a copy of Alexander Mackenzie's book with them.

Sir Alexander Mackenzie died on March 12, 1820, at Mulinearn, near Dunkeld, Scotland. He was survived by his wife and three children.

EXPEDITIONS OF COLTER AND PIKE (1804–1809)

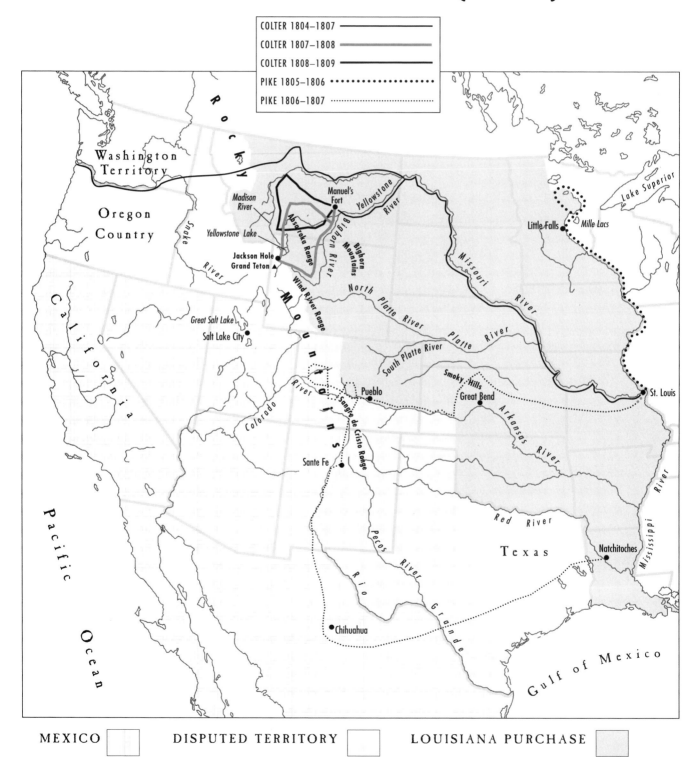

COLTER 1804–1807 ——————
COLTER 1807–1808 ——————
COLTER 1808–1809 ——————
PIKE 1805–1806 ••••••••••••
PIKE 1806–1807 ·············

Washington Territory

Oregon Country

Rocky

Madison River

Yellowstone Lake

Manuel's Fort

Yellowstone River

Absaroka Range

Bighorn River

Bighorn Mountains

Jackson Hole
Grand Teton

Wind River Range

Snake River

Mountains

North Platte River

Platte River

South Platte River

Missouri River

Little Falls

Mille Lacs

Lake Superior

St. Louis

Great Salt Lake
Salt Lake City

California

Colorado River

Sangre de Cristo Range

Pueblo

Smoky Hills
Great Bend

Arkansas River

Sante Fe

Red River

Pecos River

Rio Grande

Texas

Natchitoches

Mississippi River

Chihuahua

Pacific Ocean

Gulf of Mexico

MEXICO   DISPUTED TERRITORY   LOUISIANA PURCHASE

CHAPTER 2
Exploring the Louisiana Purchase

In January 1803, President Thomas Jefferson asked Congress to authorize an exploring expedition up the Missouri River to the Rocky Mountains and then west to the Pacific Ocean.

The region was known as Louisiana and did not belong to the United States. The territory from the Mississippi River to the Rocky Mountains belonged to France. The territory from the Rocky Mountains to the Pacific Ocean was disputed among Russia, Spain, Great Britain, and the United States.

At the time, a war was about to erupt between France and Great Britain. Rather than allow the British to capture Louisiana through war, France suddenly offered to sell Louisiana to the United States. When the treaty was signed on April 30, 1803, the United States paid France fifteen million dollars for 529,911,680 acres. The Louisiana Purchase was a great real estate deal for the United States.

While the United States had purchased more than 800,000 square miles of land, the Native American peoples who already lived on that land knew nothing of the sale. Most of the tribes did not understand land ownership in the same way as the white men. To them, land was community property. They did not believe land could be owned, just as air or the oceans could not be owned. "Mother Earth," whom they considered sacred, provided all their needs. How could anyone own "Mother Earth"? The purchase of Louisiana brought great change for both the Native Americans and the European Americans.

Congress approved Thomas Jefferson's exploring expedition to the Pacific Ocean. It became one of the most famous expeditions in history: Lewis and

Thomas Jefferson was the third president of the United States when he signed the Louisiana Purchase, which doubled the size of the new nation. Jefferson was the greatest supporter of western expansion, but surprisingly he never traveled farther west than Harpers Ferry, in what is now West Virginia.

Clark's Corps of Discovery. Led by Captains Meriwether Lewis and William Clark, the twenty-six men and one dog left St. Louis, Missouri, on May 14, 1804, in three well-supplied boats. One of the men on the expedition was John Colter, who later made one of North America's most amazing exploratory treks all by himself.

Other exploring expeditions followed Lewis and Clark's. One was led by Zebulon M. Pike, and thirteen years after Pike returned, Stephen H. Long led a group of scientists to the Rocky Mountains.

The gates to the West were beginning to open.

JOHN COLTER (1774 OR 1775-1813)

Member of the Lewis and Clark Expedition; First Mountain Man; Trapper;
Explorer; First White Man to See Jackson's Hole, the Tetons, and Parts of
Yellowstone National Park; First White Man to Cross Wind River Range

On March 1, 1872, President Ulysses S. Grant signed a bill making Yellowstone
National Park the United States' first national park.

It had been sixty-five years since John Colter originally saw the amazing

No portrait has ever been found of John Colter, but the painting above is probably
the most accurate representation of his five-hundred-mile trek alone through the wilderness
during the winter of 1807–1808. Colter's gun is held high to indicate he comes in peace.
His left hand is saying he wants to "talk" in sign language. The painting, entitled
Colter Visits the Crow—1807, is by contemporary artist John F. Clymer. Only a portion of
the painting, which belongs to the Clymer Museum of Art, is shown here.

sights of Yellowstone. He was the first known white man to see the area, but when he reported his discoveries, no one believed him. People thought he had been alone in the wilderness too long. Or maybe he was just telling tales. They referred to his imagined sites as Colter's Hell.

Born near Staunton, Virginia, in 1774 or 1775, Colter was twenty-nine years old when Meriwether Lewis went down the Ohio River recruiting men for the Corps of Discovery. When Lewis stopped in Maysville, Kentucky, on October 15, 1803, John Colter was one of the first to enlist. Colter had the necessary qualifications: "good hunter, stout, healthy, unmarried, accustomed to the woods, and capable of bearing bodily fatigue in a pretty considerable degree." Being able to read and

As a member of the Lewis and Clark Expedition, Colter was one of the hunters, a position of honor. This illustration was included in Patrick Gass's journal and shows Captain Clark and his men, one of whom is probably John Colter.

write was not required, but Colter was probably literate—two documents have been found with his signature, and he owned three books when he died.

The Corps of Discovery was a military detachment, and Colter enlisted as a private at the salary of five dollars per month. At first he was not a model soldier. In February 1804, Colter and three other men disobeyed orders and were punished. Afterward, Colter became one of the Corps' most reliable members.

The expedition left Camp Dubois near St. Louis on May 14, 1804, and proceeded up the Missouri River. Colter proved to be responsible and was often trusted with difficult or hazardous assignments.

The Lewis and Clark Expedition lasted almost two years. On their return in August 1806, the party met two men from Illinois near the Mandan villages on the upper Missouri River. Forrest Hancock and Joseph Dixon were heading into the wilderness to trap beaver. Colter's knowledge of the region would be very valuable, so they asked him to guide them.

Colter received permission to leave the Corps early, and he joined Hancock and Dixon. The three trapped beaver that winter in present-day Montana, but they ended their partnership in the spring.

In June 1807, Colter built a canoe and headed down the Missouri River to return to St. Louis. At the mouth of the Platte River, he saw two keelboats. He went ashore and was greeted by over fifty trappers, including George Drouillard, John Potts, and Peter Weiser, who were old friends from the Lewis and Clark Expedition.

Colter met the group's leader, Manuel Lisa, and learned the men were on their way to trap beaver and trade for beaver pelts with the Native American tribes. Lisa convinced Colter to join the expedition.

Colter had not returned to St. Louis since he had left with Lewis and Clark in May 1804. Now, three years later, he again decided to postpone returning to civilization.

On the trip up the Missouri River, the group narrowly escaped trouble with the Arikaras, the Mandans, and the Assiniboines. They arrived at the confluence of the Yellowstone and Bighorn rivers on November 21, 1807, and built a fort, which was usually called Manuel's Fort or Fort Lisa.

Since Colter was familiar with the area and had learned some of the local Native American languages, Lisa sent him out to invite the tribes to bring their beaver pelts to trade at his fort. Colter was also instructed to find beaver streams where Lisa's men could trap.

The next few months of Colter's life were unbelievable: He carried only his gun, some ammunition, and a thirty-pound pack of supplies and presents for the native peoples. Alone, he crossed mountain ranges on foot during the coldest and snowiest months of the year. What Colter discovered was amazing.

Historians have difficulty tracing his travels because Colter left no written records. The route he took has been determined only from Native American trails which he is known to have used, and accounts in other people's journals. Colter also told William Clark about some of his travels when he finally returned to St. Louis in 1810.

As Colter walked through the wilderness during the winter of 1807–1808, he met with many tribes. He had probably learned how to make and use snowshoes during the previous winter when he was with Dixon and Hancock. It is possible a Crow brave guided Colter in some of the confusing and difficult mountain areas.

Colter carried gifts—awls, beads, vermillion, needles, knives, and tobacco—which he exchanged for food, clothing, and lodging during his journey.

Having no horse, Colter walked five hundred miles through present-day Wyoming, Montana, and Idaho. He crossed the Pryor Mountains, the Bighorn Basin, and the Wind River Range. He endured the fierce winter, wading through deep snow. He was the first white man known to see Jackson's Hole, the Teton Range, and Pierre's Hole. It is believed he explored the falls, canyons, and headwaters of the Yellowstone River, and parts of what is today Yellowstone National Park.

When he returned to Manuel's Fort in the spring of 1808, Colter told the other trappers about the enormous mountain ranges, steaming geysers, hot springs, and boiling mud cauldrons he had seen. When they heard about the "inferno," the other trappers thought he was making it up. They laughed at his stories and thereafter referred to the region as Colter's Hell.

A few weeks later, Colter was guiding about eight hundred Flatheads and Crow to Manuel's Fort when they were attacked by fifteen hundred Blackfeet. Colter was shot in the leg, but he crawled to a thicket and continued to battle. When the fighting ended, Colter, with a serious leg wound, walked the rest of the way to Manuel's Fort—a distance of several hundred miles.

In the fall of 1808, Colter and John Potts were trapping in Blackfoot territory, so they stayed out of sight during the daytime. Early one morning, they were taking up their traps on the Jefferson River when a war party of eight hundred Blackfeet confronted them.

Colter assumed the Blackfeet intended to rob them, so he dropped his traps into the water without anyone noticing. Traps were the mountain man's only way of making a living.

The Blackfeet were feared by everyone who visited the West. The conflicts began when a member of the Lewis and Clark Expedition killed a Piegan Blackfoot in 1806. John Colter's first known battle with the Blackfeet was in the spring of 1808.

The chiefs ordered the two men to come ashore. Colter obeyed, but Potts remained in the canoe. The Blackfeet took Colter's weapons and stripped him entirely naked. Colter told Potts that he should come ashore, but Potts refused.

A brave shot Potts in the hip, and Potts dropped to the bottom of his canoe. "Colter, I am wounded," he said. Then he came back up with his rifle and killed one of the Blackfeet. Immediately the warriors killed Potts. Colter later said Potts was pierced with so many arrows that "he was made a riddle of."

The relatives of the dead warrior were furious and wanted to kill Colter, but other members of the tribe held them back.

Colter believed he would be killed at any moment. The tribe held a council to decide what to do with him.

A chief asked Colter if he could run fast. Colter responded that he was a slow runner. The chief pointed to the prairie and, using the Crow language, told Colter to leave. When he turned his back to walk toward the prairie, Colter expected to be shot.

Using sign language an old man told him to go faster. Colter heard the war whoops and glanced around. The younger braves were removing their blankets, leggings, and clothing as if they were preparing for a race. Colter realized he was to race with them, and his life and scalp would be their prize.

Naked and barefoot, Colter ran through the rocks, sagebrush, and prickly pear cacti. The young warriors were close behind him, carrying spears and yelling their war whoops.

Colter was about five miles from the Madison Fork River. He ran as fast as he could across the prairie. He even surprised himself at his speed.

After running almost three miles, blood began to gush from his nose. He glanced behind him and saw that he was ahead of all the Blackfeet except one. Colter continued running, and the blood from his nose covered the front of his body. About a mile from the Madison Fork, he heard footsteps right behind him. He expected to feel the spear at any moment.

Colter stopped suddenly and whirled around. The Blackfoot was probably startled by Colter's bloody face and body. The brave tried to throw his spear, but he lost his balance and fell. The spear broke, and Colter grabbed the

This image illustrates Colter's amazing escape from the Blackfeet in 1808.

pointed end and stabbed the brave with it. Then he pulled the point out of the dying man's body and took it with him.

Colter ran on. He heard the other Blackfeet howling and yelling when they found their fellow warrior stabbed. They were furious and continued the chase.

Colter reached the bank of the Madison Fork. He plunged into the water and swam to a place where logs had jammed and were lodged together. He dived beneath the logs and found a place where he could get his head above water but still be hidden by the timber.

He had barely hidden himself when the Blackfeet arrived at the riverbank. Later, when Colter described the incident, he said they were yelling "like so many devils."

Colter stayed very still while the warriors searched for him. They crawled onto the logs on top of where he was hiding. He could see them, but no one spotted him.

The Blackfeet searched all day, but Colter remained hidden beneath the logs in the freezing water with only his face above the surface. When night fell, the tribe left.

When Colter was certain he was safe, he swam out from under the logs and went ashore in the darkness. There was only one ravine out of the valley. It was about thirty miles away. But the Blackfeet would probably be guarding the pass. He couldn't risk going that way.

The only other escape was to climb the mountain before him, which stretched almost straight up and down. Later, when other men saw it, they judged it would be impossible for anyone, even a mountain goat, to climb. With no other choice, Colter began climbing. He grabbed rocks, tree branches, shrubs—anything that would help him pull himself to the top.

It took him all night, but by morning he had reached the top of the mountain. He stayed hidden through the next day, and that night he descended the other side.

When he reached the open plains, he headed for Manuel's Fort on the Bighorn, which was about three hundred miles away. He had escaped being killed, but he was naked, and the bottoms of his feet were punctured with prickly pear cactus thorns. While he saw plenty of game, he had only the stolen spear point, which was not large enough for hunting. He found a root to eat called a ground apple (the *Psoralea esculenta*), and he also ate the inside layer of some tree bark.

It took him eleven days to get to the fort. By then, he was extremely thin, his beard was long and matted, his feet were swollen, and because he was naked, his entire body was cut and blistered. When he first arrived, even his friends didn't recognize him.

Exhausted, Colter rested for several weeks.

Later that winter, Colter wanted to retrieve his traps from the Jefferson River. Assuming the Blackfeet would be in winter quarters, he returned to the site where Potts had been killed and made a campfire. Suddenly, he heard leaves crackling. He leaped away just as shots struck all around him. He had once again barely escaped being killed.

On April 12, 1810, Colter's trapping party encountered another band of Blackfeet. Five trappers were killed, but Colter escaped. Legend says he returned to Manuel's Fort, threw his hat to the ground, and said, "If God will only forgive me this time and let me off I will leave the country day after to-morrow—and be damned if I ever come into it again!"

Colter and William Bryan left the wilderness April 22, 1810, in a canoe. They paddled three thousand miles downriver and arrived in St. Louis only thirty days later.

Colter never returned to the mountains.

William Clark kept a map of the West that he updated as various parties reported their discoveries. Colter told Clark about some of his travels, including the tar pits and thermal springs on the upper Shoshone River near today's Cody, Wyoming. Clark's map did not mention geysers. If Colter saw geysers, perhaps he did not report them to Clark. Or if he told Clark, perhaps Clark thought Colter was imagining things.

Colter married a woman who is identified only as Sally. They had one son. John Colter died of jaundice in November 1813. When his personal possessions were sold, they brought $124.44 1/2.

John Colter was the first mountain man, and he became the model for those who followed. He chose to travel alone, and his routes turned out to be among the most difficult and dangerous in the history of the West. But because he kept no journals and left no written records, he received little credit for his incredible journeys.

ZEBULON MONTGOMERY PIKE (1779-1813)
U.S. Army Officer, Explorer of the Upper Mississippi River and the Southwest United States, Discoverer of Pikes Peak

One day in the fall of 1807, President Thomas Jefferson got a surprise: Two grizzly bear cubs were delivered to him as a gift from Zebulon Montgomery Pike.

By the time President Jefferson received the two cubs, they were over six months old and still growing! The bears had traveled from Colorado south to Chihuahua (Mexico), across Texas, and then by boat to Virginia and Jefferson's doorstep. The following January, Jefferson donated the bears to a museum.

Zebulon Montgomery Pike's name is linked to the famous Colorado mountain Pikes Peak.

Zebulon Montgomery Pike was born in Lamberton (now part of Trenton), New Jersey, on January 5, 1779. He was the second of eight children, although four of his siblings died in infancy. His father was an army major.

As a boy, Zebulon attended country schools. He entered the military at the age of fifteen as a cadet under his father's command. With books, Zebulon taught himself science, Spanish, French, mathematics, and military tactics. At the age of twenty, he was commissioned as a lieutenant. He married his cousin Clarissa Brown when he was twenty-two.

First Expedition: 1805–1806

In 1805 General James Wilkinson sent Zebulon Pike on an expedition to find the source of the Mississippi River. His three "scientific" instruments included a thermometer, a watch, and a theodolite, which is a device to determine latitude.

Pike's assignment included collecting information about the weather, natural resources, and possible sites for military posts. He was to learn how many Native Americans lived in the region, to which tribes they belonged, and with whom they traded. He was to get their consent to build forts, and invite the chiefs to St. Louis to meet with General Wilkinson.

Pike left Fort Belle Fontaine near St. Louis on August 9, 1805. Traveling with twenty enlisted men in a seventy-foot keelboat, Pike took only four months' worth of supplies. He also took gifts for the Native Americans, including tobacco, knives, whiskey, handkerchiefs, and calico and woolen cloth.

On September 23, Pike met with some Sioux chiefs and made a treaty granting the U.S. government 100,000 acres of land. In exchange, Pike gave the Sioux two hundred dollars' worth of trade goods. Fort St. Anthony, later named Fort Snelling, was built there in 1820. It is the site of today's Minneapolis and St. Paul, Minnesota.

This painting, by Titian Ramsay Peale, illustrates the two grizzly bear cubs Zebulon Pike acquired in the Rocky Mountains. The caged bears rode on the back of a mule from the Rocky Mountains into Spanish Mexico; across today's Texas to Natchitoches, Louisiana; and finally to the Virginia home of Thomas Jefferson, who then donated them to Charles Willson Peale's museum. Peale's son, Titian, who was almost nine years old when the bears arrived at his father's museum, was later a member of Stephen H. Long's expedition to the Rocky Mountains.

The party continued north, but when winter weather set in during the middle of October, they built a stockade near today's Little Falls, Minnesota. The men also built canoes and sledges. Unfazed by the severe weather, Pike left on December 10 with an exploring party of twelve men.

Almost immediately, accidents plagued the group. On December 14 a sledge overturned, dumping their gear into the river. The greatest loss was that some of their ammunition was ruined.

Three weeks later, a fire destroyed Pike's tent, clothing, and blankets. Pike wrote it was "no trivial misfortune in such a country and on such a voyage." Luckily, three casks of gunpowder did not blow up in the fire, or he would have been killed. A week later, a tree fell on one of the men and almost killed him.

On February 1, 1806, Pike concluded that Cass Lake was the source of the Mississippi River. Actually, he was wrong. The true source of the Mississippi River is Lake Itasca.

As Pike visited British trading posts, he objected to their flying the British flag. At one post, Pike had his men shoot it down and raise the United States flag.

The exploring group returned to the stockade at the end of March, and the entire expedition left on April 7 to return to St. Louis. They arrived on April 30, having traveled more than five thousand miles.

On this expedition, Pike did not discover anything, and none of the chiefs traveled to St. Louis to meet General Wilkinson. Pike thought he had established peace between the tribes, but the Sioux and the Chippewa were soon at war.

Although Pike's maps and journals contained errors, his trip gave the United States a basis to claim Minnesota in later land disputes with the British.

Second Expedition: 1806–1807

Less than three months later, Pike received his next assignment. He was to return some Osage people to their homes, negotiate peace between the Kansas and Osage tribes, and find the headwaters of the Arkansas River and the Red River, which was the boundary dividing the United States and Spanish Mexico.

Pike was to record the region's minerals, plants, animals, natural history, geography, and geology. If he encountered the Spanish, he was to "prevent alarm or offence."

But the mission was clouded by a conspiracy. One of the men involved was General Wilkinson, who, in addition to being Pike's commanding officer, was also governor of the Louisiana Territory and head of the United States Army. The other man was Aaron Burr, a former vice president. The two men planned to take over much of today's southwestern United States, but they needed more information: How difficult was travel in Mexico? How many forts were there? Where were they located? How many troops were assigned to the forts?

To make the situation even stranger, Wilkinson was a double agent. He was being paid by the Spanish for information about American exploration in the Southwest. Wilkinson ordered Pike to explore near Spanish territory, but he also informed the Spanish that Pike was on his way, knowing they would arrest him. Wilkinson must have known Pike's arrest would enable him to spy in what is today New Mexico.

It is suspected that Wilkinson gave Pike secret instructions to spy, but Pike probably did not know about Wilkinson and Burr's takeover scheme.

Pike left Fort Belle Fontaine on July 15, 1806, accompanied by Lieutenant James B. Wilkinson (General Wilkinson's son), nineteen military men, Baroney Vasquez (an interpreter), Dr. John H. Robinson, and fifty-one Osage people who had been captured by the Potawatomi and then released to the United States military.

It took a month to reach Grand Osage, near today's Missouri-Kansas border. Pike obtained horses from the Osage and moved on to the Pawnee villages near today's Kansas-Nebraska line. He stayed two weeks, holding council with the chiefs and trying to make peace among the Osage, Kansas, and Pawnee tribes.

When Pike first arrived, his party received a warm welcome, but six hundred Spanish soldiers, with their two thousand horses and mules, had just visited the Pawnee. Obviously, the Pawnee respected the large Spanish army more than Pike's twenty poorly equipped soldiers. The chief told Pike he had promised to stop any Americans from traveling across the plains. Pike refused to back down. On October 7, he and his men left the Pawnee villages and continued on. They were ready to fight, but the Pawnee did not pursue them.

Traveling across present-day
Colorado on November 15, 1806,
Pike saw the mountain that
today is known as
Pikes Peak.

Pike's party went south to the Arkansas River near today's Great Bend, Kansas, where Lieutenant Wilkinson took five enlisted men and returned to St. Louis. Pike took sixteen men and the horses and went west, following the Arkansas River.

They saw large herds of wild horses and elk. One buffalo herd covered the entire prairie as far as they could see. On November 15, Pike saw a mountain that appeared like "a small blue cloud." That mountain was later named Pikes Peak.

The men's horses were becoming weak from a lack of good grazing. When snow began to fall, the horses' only food was leaves and the bark of cottonwood trees.

On November 22, a band of sixty Pawnee warriors surrounded the party. They pretended to be friendly, but suddenly three Pawnee jumped on three of Pike's horses and rode away. Luckily, the horses were soon returned.

Pike gave fire steels and flints to each warrior, and tobacco and knives to the chiefs. They accepted the gifts, but then tossed them aside and demanded ammunition, corn, blankets, and kettles. Pike indicated he had no more gifts. Tensions were high. Pike's sixteen men were greatly outnumbered. Finally, the Pawnee accepted their presents. They also stole some other items, but the two groups parted without any shots being fired.

The next day, the men set up camp near today's Pueblo, Colorado. That afternoon, Pike, Dr. Robinson, Private Miller, and Private Brown set out to climb Grand Peak, the mountain now known as Pikes Peak. Pike thought it would only be a day's hike.

After two days, they reached the base of what is now known as Cheyenne

In November 1806, Pike and three of his men tried unsuccessfully to climb the mountain
that would later be named Pikes Peak.

Mountain. They killed a deer and hung it in a tree so that they would have meat on their return. They also left their blankets at the base of the mountain, thinking that the climb would take only a few hours.

But the climb was steep and difficult. That night they were not yet at the top of Cheyenne Mountain. They slept in a rock-filled cave without food, water, or blankets. Pike had made a serious mistake: When the expedition left St. Louis, they carried no warm clothes, only lightweight cotton uniforms. Even worse, they were not wearing socks.

The next morning, their thermometer read four degrees below zero. The four men stood in snow to their waists, yet they were astounded by the "sublime" view of the prairie and mountains.

It took an hour to reach the top of Cheyenne Mountain. From there, Grand Peak appeared to be twice as high as the mountain on which they stood. Pike wrote in his journal, "I believe no human being could have ascended to its summit."

Pike wanted to climb the mountain for more than just the view. He had the false idea that all the western rivers had one common source. He believed that if he could climb high enough, he could see the lake or glacier where all the rivers originated.

When Pike's group descended the mountain, they found that animals had eaten most of the deer. Snow began to fall, and the men took cover under a projecting rock. They shared one partridge and a piece of deer's rib. It was their first food in two days.

Pike and his men returned to camp. A terrible snowstorm set in that night, but Pike insisted the expedition march the next morning. Once the storm subsided, the temperature fell to seventeen degrees below zero. Despite the cold, the party went into the mountains, and almost a week later they found the canyon now called the Royal Gorge. On December 13, they came to the South Platte River, and five days later, they reached what Pike thought was the Red River.

On Christmas Day, the party finally killed a buffalo. After not eating for two days, they enjoyed a feast. But the temperature was below zero, and the men were freezing. They cut their blankets into pieces to wrap around their feet and huddled close to the huge campfire.

They set out again the next day, but there was no grazing for the horses; the few still surviving were so weak they kept falling on the rough terrain and were almost useless.

On the morning of January 5, 1807, Pike went hunting. He fell on a hill and his gun broke off by the breech. Then a few hours later, Pike realized the river he had been following was not the Red River. It was the Arkansas. He had been going in a circle.

This was Pike's twenty-eighth birthday. Embarrassed, he wrote in his journal, "This was a great mortification. . . . This was my birth-day, and most fervently did I hope never to pass another so miserably."

The men built a stockade near today's Pueblo, Colorado. Baroney Vasquez and Patrick Smith had frozen feet, so Pike decided to leave them at the stockade with the horses.

On January 14, Pike and the other fourteen men left on foot, with each man carrying a seventy-pound pack. They went southwest through the Sangre de Cristo Mountains. A few days later, everyone's feet got wet crossing a creek. By evening, nine men had frozen feet and could no longer walk. Their thermometer registered eighteen degrees below zero, and they were out of food.

On January 18, Pike and Dr. Robinson went hunting. They injured a buffalo, but it ran off. The two refused to return to camp that evening without food for the hungry, freezing men. It was too cold to sleep, so they sat up in the rocks all night.

The next day, they saw a small buffalo herd. Again they wounded one, and it ran off. Weak and convinced they were going to die, they agreed to die alone in the woods rather than return and face the men who had entrusted their lives to Pike. Late that afternoon, Pike finally shot a buffalo. They arrived back at camp with the meat at midnight. No one had eaten for four days, so everyone stayed up all night feasting!

When it was time to leave, Thomas Dougherty's and John Sparks's feet were too frozen to walk. Pike left them behind with buffalo meat and ammunition. When the main party left, all the men wept.

Another snowstorm moved in and it was impossible to find any game. Pike and his men marched for three days in three feet of snow with nothing to eat. Late in the afternoon of the third day, Dr. Robinson finally shot another buffalo.

Once again they ate well. But the next day, Pike wrote in his journal that, for the first time on the journey, he found himself discouraged.

On January 26, Hugh Menaugh's feet froze and he remained behind. The next day, Pike followed a small stream past large hills of sand, now known as the Great Sand Dunes. His men built a stockade on a tributary of the nearby river.

On February 7, Pike sent a group of soldiers back to get the men who had been left behind at various camps.

Near the end of February, a hundred Spanish soldiers arrived at the stockade. They offered to provide horses and mules and guide Pike's party to the Red River. Pike said, "What, is not this the Red River?" The Spanish commander responded, "No, sir, it is the Rio del Norte," today's Rio Grande. Pike acted bewildered and ordered his men to take down the American flag. He agreed to go to Santa Fe to meet the Spanish governor.

Pike and his men are portrayed being taken to Santa Fe by Spanish troops in this picture by Frederic Remington, painted almost a hundred years after the actual event.

Pike said he thought he was on the Red River, but he surely knew where he was and only pretended to be lost. General Wilkinson probably secretly instructed Pike to spy in Santa Fe. If Pike only wanted to find the Red River, he would have accepted the offer of horses, mules, and the escort.

Half the Spanish soldiers stayed behind to rescue the rest of Pike's men from the mountains. Pike and his men at the stockade were taken to Santa Fe. Governor Joaquin del Real Alencaster questioned Pike and examined his notes and maps. He assigned Lieutenant Don Facundo Melgares to escort the Americans to Chihuahua for further questioning.

Melgares and Pike became good friends on the journey. As they traveled, the local villagers entertained the group with dinners and dances. Pike described the people as having "heaven-like qualities of hospitality and kindness."

In Chihuahua, Governor Don Nemesio Salcedo questioned Pike and took his papers. After several weeks, the governor was convinced Pike was a spy, but he decided not to take action that would anger the American government. Instead he wrote letters of protest to American officials, and reported the incident to his superiors in Spain. The governor ordered Lieutenant Melgares to escort Pike and his men back tzo the United States. They left Chihuahua on April 28. Even on the trip, Pike made notes and hid them in the barrels of his men's rifles. Pike was released in Natchitoches, Louisiana, on July 1, 1807.

While he was gone, Pike had been promoted to captain. But he was also suspected of being part of the Burr-Wilkinson conspiracy scandal, which had been exposed in the late summer and fall of 1806. Pike wrote to General Henry Dearborn, the secretary of war, denying that he was involved. Dearborn accepted Pike's explanation.

Pike had made careful observations, though much of his report was written from memory. Pike's comments, along with observations by Major Stephen Long in 1820, perpetuated the myth that the Great Plains were the "Great American Desert."

As an officer in the United States Army, Pike was dedicated, patriotic, and brave. But as an explorer, he made some unwise decisions. Instead of building a fort to winter in, he ordered his men to march in freezing temperatures without

In 1808, Pike was promoted to the rank of major in the United States Army. He fought the British at York in the War of 1812, and died from wounds he received when a British storehouse full of ammunition exploded. His last words were, "Push on, my brave fellows."

proper clothing and often without food. He never expected more from his men than he expected of himself, but he put his troops in dangerous situations that could have killed the entire party. Several of the men had lost parts of their feet to frostbite.

Nevertheless, Pike and his men risked their lives under orders of the United States Army. Yet, the government did not give Pike's men extra pay or grants of land, as they had rewarded the members of the Lewis and Clark Expedition.

Pike remained in the military and was killed in the War of 1812. He died April 27, 1813. He was thirty-four years old.

STEPHEN HARRIMAN LONG (1784-1864)

Explorer of the Mississippi, Minnesota, and Western United States Rivers;
Discoverer of Longs Peak; Surveyor; U.S. Army Officer and Engineer

Odd. Strange. Very unusual.

In fact, all those people standing on the Ohio River bank on that May afternoon in 1819 might have used more colorful language as they watched the steamboat move past. Named the *Western Engineer,* it was certainly not an average steamboat. Designed by Major Stephen H. Long, it was intended to impress the Native Americans living on the upper Mississippi and Missouri rivers.

The boat appeared to ride on the back of a large black sea monster. At the bow, the serpent's scaly, reptile-like head rose out of the water as high as the boat's deck. The engine's steam and smoke belched from the monster's mouth. In the rear, the paddle wheel churned the water, and it appeared that the monster was thrashing and creating waves.

When some Native Americans saw the boat in St. Louis, one said, "White man bad man, keep a great spirit chained and build fire under it to make it work a boat."

Stephen H. Long was born in Hopkinton, New Hampshire, on December 30, 1784. He was the second child in a family of thirteen children. After graduating from Dartmouth College in 1809, he worked as a teacher in New Hampshire, then as a school principal in Pennsylvania. In 1815, he became a professor of mathematics at the military academy now known as West Point. The next year he was one of the first six officers in the newly formed Army Corps of Topographical Engineers.

First Expedition: 1817

In 1817, Long led an exploration expedition to the northern frontier, in what is now Minnesota and Wisconsin. The army planned to build several forts there, and Long was to select appropriate sites. He was also to gather information on natural resources, geography, geology, natural history, and Native American peoples.

He left Fort Belle Fontaine near St. Louis, Missouri, on June 1, 1817, in a six-

EXPEDITIONS OF LONG (1817–1823)

LONG 1817	——————
LONG 1819–1820	——————
LONG 1823	• • • • • •

MEXICO ☐   DISPUTED TERRITORY ☐   LOUISIANA PURCHASE ☐

Stephen Harriman Long's explorations covered over 26,000 miles, more than three times the distance covered by Lewis and Clark.

oared skiff borrowed from William Clark. His party of fifteen men traveled up the Mississippi River to the Falls of St. Anthony, present-day Minneapolis and St. Paul, Minnesota. They went up the Wisconsin River and returned to Fort Belle Fontaine on August 15, after a seventy-five-day expedition.

On Long's recommendation, the army built several forts, including Fort St. Anthony, later called Fort Snelling.

Second Expedition: 1819-1820

Before leaving on his 1817 expedition, Long had proposed to the War Department that he design and build a steamboat to explore the upper Missouri River. In 1818 Long's proposal was approved as part of the Yellowstone Expedition, which consisted of a military division headed by General Henry Atkinson and a scientific expedition under Long.

Long designed the steamboat, named it the *Western Engineer*, and oversaw its

When Long's steamboat, the *Western Engineer*, arrived at Council Bluffs (now known as Fort Atkinson, Nebraska), it was the first steamboat to successfully travel that far on the Missouri River. This image of the *Western Engineer* was done by Cornelius Ismert.

construction. It left Pittsburgh, Pennsylvania, on May 5, 1819, and arrived in St. Louis on June 9.

Meanwhile, General Atkinson moved one thousand troops up the Missouri River in four steamboats. These were the first steamboats ever used on the Missouri, and they were plagued with accidents, delays, low water levels, and mud. After the troops reached Old Council Bluffs, in present-day Nebraska, most of the men were seriously ill with scurvy and fever, and one hundred sixty of them died.

Long's scientific expedition arrived on September 17, 1819, and the men built winter quarters five miles below Old Council Bluffs. They called it Engineer Cantonment.

Over the winter, the War Department changed the Yellowstone Expedition's assignment. The military troops were to proceed no farther than Old Council Bluffs. The scientific division was to use horses to cross the plains and find the source of the Platte, Arkansas, and Red rivers.

As Major Long and his men prepared for their journey, local Native Americans predicted they would not find enough water, game, or grazing for the horses. Baroney Vasquez, who had been Zebulon Pike's interpreter, warned of hostile tribes that might attack.

Ignoring the warnings, Long set off on June 6, 1820, with twenty-two men, including John Bell, journalist; Edwin James, botanist, geologist, and surgeon; Titian Peale, assistant naturalist; Thomas Say, zoologist and ethnologist; Samuel Seymour, landscape artist; William Swift, assistant topographer and commander of escort; as well as interpreters, guides, hunters, baggage handlers, and military men.

Besides their provisions, weapons, and equipment, the party's scientific instruments included several compasses, a portable horizon, two sextants, and two thermometers. They also took goods to trade with the Native Americans,

This picture by Samuel Seymour, a member of Long's party, was made as the expedition moved up the Missouri River in 1819. It is entitled *War Dance in the Interiour of a Konza Lodge.*

A Government Pack Train was painted by Frederic Remington in the late nineteenth century. The report of Long's expedition indicated they were delayed in the first few days of their journey by the inexperience of many of their men.
The scene probably looked a lot like this!

such as vermillion, small metal bells, beads, combs, scissors, awls, looking glasses, knives, fire steels, tobacco, and flints.

During the first few days, they experienced delays caused by obstinate mules, inexperienced men, mosquitoes, and a violent thunder storm that soaked everything.

On June 11, the party arrived at the Village of the Grand Pawnees. Chief Long Hair said, "You must have long hearts, to undertake such a journey with so weak a force; hearts that would reach from the earth to the heavens."

The next day, they moved to the Village of the Republican Pawnees, named for the nearby Republican River. Chief Fool Robe met with the men, but he was not welcoming.

At the third Pawnee village, Knife-Chief rode out a mile to greet Long's party. They didn't need an interpreter to tell he was glad to see them. He treated them as guests, serving them sweet corn. Knife-Chief also warned, "Your heart must be strong to go upon so hazardous a journey. May the Master of Life be your protector." All three Pawnee chiefs discouraged the journey, but Long suspected they were protecting their hunting grounds.

Long's party followed the Platte River west through what is now Nebraska and Colorado. The scientists collected data, made astronomical and weather observations, and recorded the insects, plants, and animals they found. They noted the practice of the rattlesnake occupying the prairie dog's hole.

On June 20, a dog joined their camp. They already had one dog, a large mastiff named Caesar, but the animals were valuable as companions and guards.

Samuel Seymour made this drawing of the expedition on the Great Plains.

The party spotted the Rocky Mountains on June 30. The highest peak they saw was later named Longs Peak.

South of present-day Denver, they camped near a creek. A heavy rain fell, and huge amounts of buffalo dung floated downstream. By the time the water rose six feet, the men could not see the creek for the dung. Captain John Bell described the stench as "intolerable."

The next day, Dr. James took two men with him to climb the mountain Pike had called Grand Peak. The climb was more difficult than James had anticipated, and by dark, the three men were perched on the side of the mountain with no level ground on which to sleep. They wedged a pole between two trees to keep from sliding down the mountain.

Late the next afternoon, they reached the top, making them the first white men to climb the mountain that would later be named Pikes Peak. Their biggest surprise was "clouds" of grasshoppers so thick that they obscured the sunlight.

Since Dr. James was the first person to climb the peak, Long named it James Peak. The name was changed to Pikes Peak in 1835, but another peak in Colorado was later named James Peak.

The expedition moved south to the Arkansas River, and Dr. James, Captain Bell, Abraham Ledoux, and William Parish explored what is now called the Royal Gorge.

On July 21, near present-day Rocky Ford, Colorado, the expedition met a Kaskaia warrior named Buffalo Calf and his wife. Buffalo Calf told Long that six tribal nations were meeting together farther down the Arkansas River, where they had battled with the Spaniards. This explained why Long's party had not met even one Native American since they had left the Pawnee villages.

On July 24, Long's expedition divided into two groups.

Captain Bell's Contingency Descending the Arkansas River

Captain Bell took eleven men and followed the Arkansas River. Two days later, they met a party of five hundred Arapaho, Kiowa, Cheyenne, and Kaskaia. A group of the men came running to welcome them. They shook hands, and the women brought jerked buffalo meat. The Native Americans called the explorers Tabbyboos.

This sketch of Long's meeting with the Nebraska Pawnees, entitled *Pawnee Council,* was drawn by Samuel Seymour. Major Long is one of the men sitting in front of his tent, listening to the Pawnee chiefs.

The men, women, and children were fascinated by the expedition's equipment and curious about the horseshoes on the horses. An elderly man asked to examine Bell's skin, since he had never seen a white man before.

Bell met with the chiefs in his tent the next morning. In order to hold council, Bell spoke in English to Stephen Julian. Julian translated the message in French to Abraham Ledoux. Ledoux spoke in Pawnee to a Native American who had been a Pawnee prisoner. That man interpreted the message into the languages of the chiefs.

All the people crowded in to hear what was being said. The children were mounted on horses—three or four to a horse. Some knelt or stood on the backs of the horses.

The chiefs indicated they were happy to see the Americans and hoped that traders would bring goods to exchange with their tribes. Bell said that if his party was treated well, traders would soon come into their country.

The two groups separated, and on July 30, Bell met a party of nine friendly Arapaho. Two days later, they met a Cheyenne war party. The Cheyenne were painted black, wore feathers and ornaments, and carried spears, war clubs, tomahawks, and bows and arrows. Bell communicated through Joseph Bijou, who spoke the Crow language with the Cheyenne's Crow prisoner.

The Cheyenne had recently fought with the Pawnees, but they met with Bell in peace. Afterward, the chief hugged Bell, who was relieved that a much-feared war party had not taken his men's scalps.

A short time later, they met a group of thirty-five Comanches who had just been defeated by a party of Ottoes.

Bell's party encountered mosquitoes, large green flies, and rattlesnakes. But their worst problems were with heat, severe thunderstorms, and a lack of cornmeal, game, and good water. One day the twelve men had to share just one skunk. The entire party was exhausted from a lack of food.

In the middle of August, it was so hot that their dog Caesar died in the arms of one of the men. All the men mourned his death. Five days later, the other dog also died.

On August 31, the party awoke to find three men missing. The men had deserted during the night and taken everything of value—the three best horses, saddlebags, rifles and ammunition, clothing, and all the gifts for the Native Americans.

The worst loss was the expedition's records. They took the journal of the topographer, Lieutenant William H. Swift. They took all the written records of Thomas Say, the zoologist: his journal; observations and notes on the manners, habits, and history of the Native American tribes; two books of vocabularies of the Native American languages; descriptions of animals including their manners and habits; and his topographical maps, charts, and data. It was a tremendous loss. To lose so much valuable information almost destroyed the purpose of the entire expedition.

On September 1, the discouraged party met an Osage man. He felt so sorry for the ragged, half-starved group that he gave them plums from his pack and said he would return. At sunset, he and five friends returned with a large deer, which they cooked for Bell's group. When the Osage learned of the desertion of the three men and the theft, they were as indignant as the members of the expedition.

The party went on to Belle Point, which later became Fort Smith, Arkansas. They offered a reward, but neither the three men nor the manuscripts were ever found.

Bell's group waited at Belle Point for Long's party.

Major Long's Contingency Descending the Red River

When Major Long and Captain Bell separated on July 24, Long took nine men with him, including Dr. Edwin James. They traveled south to find the Red River, which was the boundary between the United States and Spanish Mexico. Today the Red River is the boundary between Oklahoma and Texas.

The country was difficult to cross. The first day, the temperature rose to one hundred degrees. Their only water was stagnant puddles infested with mosquito larvae. Plodding through the muddy streambed exhausted the horses, but when they climbed out of the ravine, piles of rocks and narrow ridges nearly stopped them.

On the evening of July 27, the hunters killed a buffalo. Everyone welcomed the feast and stayed up most of the night eating and talking.

Two days later the party was pelted by rain and hail so violent that the horses refused to travel. The rain continued until evening and soaked everything. All their clothes and blankets were wet, and the men were numb with cold.

There was no wood to make a fire, and no game. Each man was rationed a mere ounce of jerked buffalo meat. Since their tent was designed for only four people, the ten men slept with their heads in the center and the lower half of their bodies sticking out from under the tent. They kept warm by crowding against one another.

With no grass to graze on, the horses were exhausted. Many were lame from the rocky ground. Day after day, the party faced the same difficulties. On August 5, they killed a wild horse that had been following them, and five days later, the hunters killed a diseased buffalo. The meat tasted terrible, but the men were too hungry to pass it up.

That afternoon, they encountered a party of two hundred fifty Bad Heart, or Comanches, with five hundred horses. Chief Red Mouse assured Long that the dry streambed they were following was the Red River.

The chief insisted that Long's party camp with them. The women erected thirty-two cone-shaped lodges, working "in perfect silence and good order." One woman erected a lodge for Long's party.

Long gave gifts to the chief, but Red Mouse was convinced they were traders out of Santa Fe and that they were hiding "better" goods in their packs. The warriors began opening the baggage until Long ordered them away. Relations soured.

The next morning, some of Long's horses and small articles were missing, but were later returned, and the two parties went in opposite directions.

For several days, the temperature rose above one hundred degrees, and the few pools of water they found were stagnant and too filthy with buffalo dung to use even for cooking. Then a hot wind came up that blew sand in their faces; it burned their eyes so badly, they could not see to guide their horses.

On August 18, they found a little water in the riverbed and a huge herd of buffalo nearby. By the following week, game became plentiful. But now they were tormented by gnats, blowflies, and ticks. The ticks burrowed beneath the men's skin and caused itching and infection. Nothing could keep them away.

Another problem was that the men and their clothing were filthy from traveling in heat, living with horses and mules, sleeping on the ground, hunting and butchering game, and cooking outdoors. All the explorers encountered the same situations, but Long and his men seemed more bothered by the conditions.

On September 10, the river they were following joined a larger river, which they knew was the Arkansas. At that point, Long realized they had been following the wrong river—it was *not* the Red River but the Canadian River.

Long was mortified.

It was too late to turn back. They had no choice but to go on to Belle Point. They joined Bell and his men on September 13.

Because of this error, historians have criticized Long. The fact that he did not know which river he was on has clouded his other accomplishments.

The report of the trip was written by Dr. Edwin James and illustrated with Samuel Seymour's sketches. It included the first dictionary of western Native American sign language.

In 1806, Zebulon Pike had indicated that the Great Plains were a "Great American Desert." Long's report perpetuated the theory when "Great Desert" was written on the map, and the text read: "In regard to this . . . country, . . . it is almost wholly unfit for cultivation, and . . . uninhabitable by a people depending upon agriculture for their subsistence. Although tracts of fertile land considerably extensive are occasionally to be met with, yet the scarcity of wood and water . . . will prove an insuperable obstacle in the way of settling the country."

All the exploration expeditions had to attend to basic cleanliness routines.
Wash day in Long's early camps must have looked very similar to this. As Long's party
moved along the muddy streambed that Long thought was the Red River, they had no water
to drink, let alone to wash clothes. The report indicates they all smelled bad!

Historians have held Long responsible for delaying the settlement of European Americans in the West. He is also criticized for never finding the sources of the Red and Platte rivers.

Third Expedition: 1823

In 1823, Long left Philadelphia on his third expedition. Thomas Say and Samuel Seymour, who had gone to the Rocky Mountains with Long, also accompanied him on this expedition.

They traveled overland to Fort Snelling and then went up the St. Peter's River, now called the Minnesota River. They crossed the portage to the headwaters of the Red River of the North.

The expedition surveyed part of the forty-ninth parallel, which is the border between the United States and Canada today. They went north to Canada's Lake Winnipeg; then southeast to Lake Superior and the Erie Canal, which was still under construction. They returned to Philadelphia on October 26, 1823.

The 1823 expedition was Long's last trip as an explorer. His explorations had covered more than twenty-six thousand miles from the Atlantic coast, as far west as the Rocky Mountains, as far south as present-day New Mexico, and north into Canada.

In the following years, Long worked as an engineer on road surveys and on the building of railroads and bridges. In 1829, he wrote the first book in the U.S. on railroad construction, entitled *Railroad Manual*. He also designed and built his own bridges.

When the Civil War started, he was promoted to colonel. Stephen Long died in Alton, Illinois, on September 4, 1864. He was survived by his wife, Martha, and five children.

CHAPTER 3
Trapping in the Wilderness

First came the beaver. Then came the warm, soft hats. Then came the opening of the West.

Around 1600, beaver hats became the height of fashion for stylish men in Europe. As people moved across the Atlantic, the fashion spread to major North American cities.

When the beaver was overtrapped in Europe and became almost extinct, those left in North America became more valuable. Men who went into the wilderness to gather beaver pelts were called mountain men. They trapped the beaver themselves or traded for pelts with Native Americans.

As the trappers scattered out, they were simply searching for better trapping areas. Actually, many mountain men were the explorers who opened the West. They made trails, discovered mountain passes, and established trading relations with Native American tribes.

A mountain man needed intelligence and skill to protect himself, provide for himself, and not get lost! He had no shelter unless he built a tepee, a lean-to, or a cabin. He ate only what he shot.

The mountain man faced every kind of danger, including starvation, thirst, extreme weather conditions, horse theft, loneliness, snow blindness, attacks by Native American peoples, insect bites, fires, grizzly bear and other wild animal attacks, diseases, infection, gunshot wounds, and other accidents.

Mountain men quickly learned that to survive in the wilderness, they would have to copy the native people's clothing, tools, shelter, food, medicine, canoes, and bullboats. Many tribes were friendly and helped the mountain men. Others

81

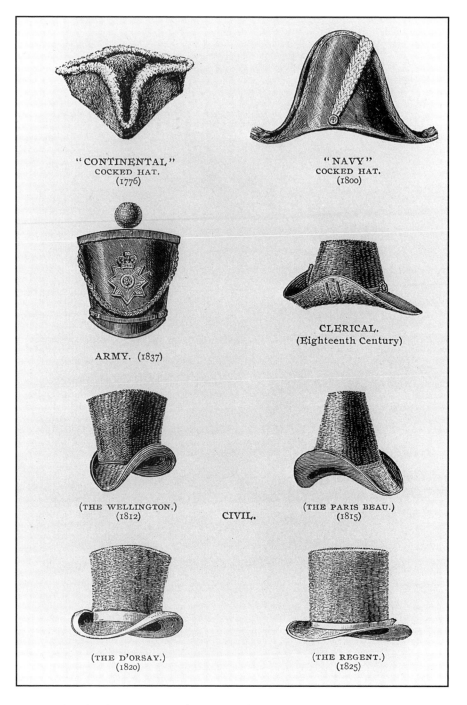

"CONTINENTAL"
COCKED HAT.
(1776)

"NAVY"
COCKED HAT.
(1800)

ARMY. (1837)

CLERICAL.
(Eighteenth Century)

(THE WELLINGTON.)
(1812)

CIVIL.

(THE PARIS BEAU.)
(1815)

(THE D'ORSAY.)
(1820)

(THE REGENT.)
(1825)

For over two hundred years, beaver hats were the height of fashion, especially for men. In fact, a beaver hat was a requirement for any gentleman appearing in public in the seventeenth, eighteenth, and first part of the nineteenth centuries, particulary in Europe. The hats came in various styles, including military fashion.

To gather beaver pelts, trappers used five to ten iron traps weighing about five pounds each. Each beaver pelt weighed from one and a half to two pounds and brought from four to six dollars a pound in St. Louis. Traders such as General William H. Ashley paid about half that amount for pelts in the mountains.

could be friendly if it was to their benefit. A few were hostile, since the white men sold weapons to their enemies, invaded their hunting grounds, and trapped more than their share of beaver.

Many mountain men married Native American women. Marrying a white man raised a native woman's status in her tribe. Plus, white husbands provided their wives with jewelry, beads, cloth, ribbon, and modern conveniences such as metal cooking pots.

In general, mountain men preferred Native American wives because of their superior skills. Native American women could make moccasins or buckskin clothing, skin and dress beaver pelts, and erect a tepee in record time. Few white women could compare.

Trapping beaver was done in the spring and fall. The trapper waded in ice-cold mountain streams to set his traps at sunset, then retrieved them at sunrise. He skinned and cleaned the pelts, and stretched them on hoops made of dried willow branches. After the pelts were dried, he folded them and bundled them together in packs.

There were two kinds of trappers. A "company trapper" received his outfit from a fur company and sold his pelts to his employer. "Free trappers" furnished their own equipment, trapped where they pleased, and sold the furs to whoever paid the most.

Mountain men were
tough, independent,
and self-sufficient.
They loved the
freedom of living
without laws and
social rules.

Some free trappers took their furs back to St. Louis themselves. But this meant risking attacks by Native Americans or boating accidents that might send the entire year's work sinking to the bottom of the river. So most sold their pelts at the forts that traders established in the wilderness.

In 1822, General William H. Ashley and Major Andrew Henry, partners in a fur trade company, ran ads in Missouri newspapers. One read:

To Enterprising Young Men

The subscriber wishes to engage ONE HUNDRED MEN, to ascend the river Missouri to its source, there to be employed for one, two or three years—For particulars, enquire of Major Andrew Henry, near the Lead Mines, in the County of Washington, (who will ascend with and command the party) or to the subscriber at St. Louis,

Wm. H. Ashley

Many "enterprising young men" responded to the ads, and over the next three years, Ashley brought out five hundred packs of pelts worth over $250,000. In 1825, Ashley decided to try a different idea. Instead of building forts or trading posts, he spread the word there would be a summer "rendezvous," which came from a French word meaning "meeting." This wasn't a new idea, but it had never been done in the Rocky Mountains before.

Boats take packs of beaver pelts down the Missouri River to sell in St. Louis.

The rendezvous was the highlight of the year for the mountain men. In this painting by Frederic Remington, the mountain men are shown rushing to the rendezvous.

That summer, Ashley brought a pack train from St. Louis to Henry's Fork, a river in Wyoming. He carried supplies such as blankets, coats, knives, traps, firearms, powder and lead, tobacco, flour, sugar, salt, tea, and coffee. He also brought goods to trade with the Native Americans, such as shawls, beads, bells, mirrors, and calico cloth. The trappers brought their pelts to the rendezvous and got resupplied for the following year.

The rendezvous became an annual summer event. The best part about it was that it was a huge party for the mountain men, the traders, and the Native Americans. There was singing, gambling, fighting, drinking, whooping, laughing, and chasing Native American women. There were contests such as wrestling, shooting, running, jumping, and horse racing. There was also a *lot* of bragging and lying, since most mountain men took pride in telling a better yarn than the next fellow.

The last rendezvous was held in 1840. By then, overtrapping had almost eliminated the beaver population. Silk hats began to overtake beaver hats in popularity, so the demand for beaver pelts dwindled. The mountain men had to find other ways to make a living. A few returned to civilization. Some farmed. Some stayed in the mountains. A few became scouts for the army or guides for wagon trains.

Only a handful, such as Jim Bridger, Jedediah Smith, and Joseph Walker, became legends.

The rendezvous was held each summer from 1825 to 1840. Most of the rendezvous were held in present-day Wyoming, although some were held in Utah and Idaho. This picture, painted by William Henry Jackson, depicts the 1837 rendezvous on the Green River.

EXPEDITIONS OF BRIDGER, SMITH, AND WALKER (1823–1867)

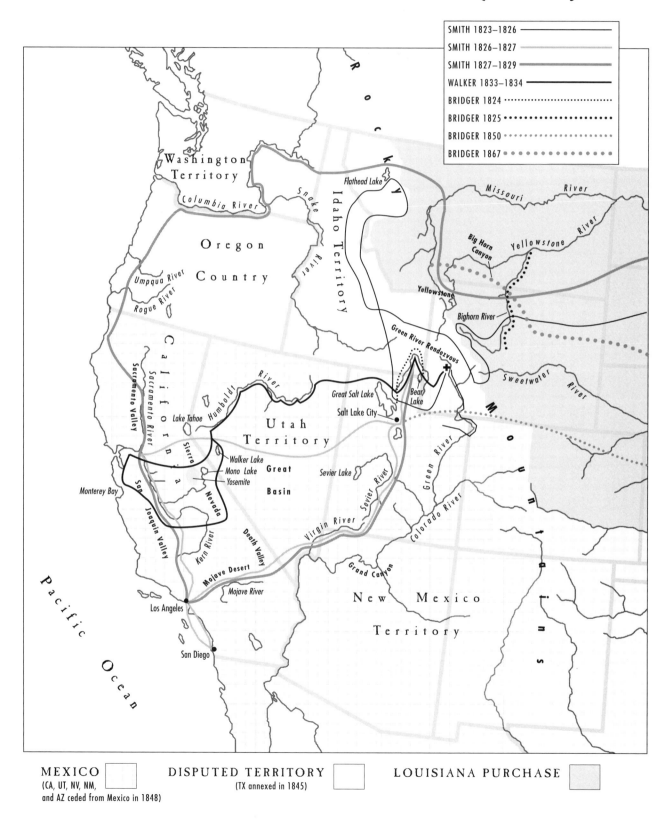

SMITH 1823–1826 ——————
SMITH 1826–1827 ——————
SMITH 1827–1829 ——————
WALKER 1833–1834 ——————
BRIDGER 1824 ·················
BRIDGER 1825 ●●●●●●●●●●●
BRIDGER 1850 ·················
BRIDGER 1867 ●●●●●●●●●●●

Washington Territory

Columbia River

Oregon Country

Umpqua River

Rogue River

Snake River

Idaho Territory

Flathead Lake

Rocky

Missouri River

Big Horn Canyon

Yellowstone River

Yellowstone

Bighorn River

Green River Rendezvous

Sweetwater River

California

Sacramento Valley

Sacramento River

Lake Tahoe

Humboldt River

Great Salt Lake

Salt Lake City

Bear Lake

Green River

Mountains

Utah Territory

Sierra

Nevada

Walker Lake
Mono Lake
Yosemite

Great Basin

Sevier Lake

Sevier River

Monterey Bay

San Joaquin Valley

Kern River

Death Valley

Mojave Desert

Mojave River

Virgin River

Grand Canyon

Colorado River

New Mexico Territory

Pacific Ocean

Los Angeles

San Diego

MEXICO
(CA, UT, NV, NM,
and AZ ceded from Mexico in 1848)

DISPUTED TERRITORY
(TX annexed in 1845)

LOUISIANA PURCHASE

JAMES BRIDGER (1804-1881)

*Mountain Man, Fur Trapper and Trader, Explorer, First White Man to Discover
Great Salt Lake, Trail Blazer, Founder of Fort Bridger, U.S. Army
Guide and Scout, Native American Interpreter*

Jim Bridger fit the description of a real mountain man, which included the art of "tellin' yarns," or stories.

Bridger often said that he had been in the mountains so long that he remembered when Pikes Peak was still a hole in the ground. Of course, that story was not true!

Bridger told about a fishing hole where he could hook a trout and then turn around and boil it just a few feet away. Amazingly, that story *was* true. The area is in present-day Yellowstone National Park.

Another tale was about "peetrified trees a-growing with peetrified birds a-singing peetrified songs." Bridger added that colored jewels grew on the "peetrified bushes" and that he had gathered a quart of them himself. He really had seen a petrified forest, minus the birds and the jewels!

Bridger often told about the time some Native American warriors surprised him and chased him on their ponies. He was armed only with a six-shooter, so he tried to escape. The first warrior closed in on him. Jim turned in his saddle and shot him. One after another they overtook him; one after another he shot them until there was only one warrior left.

They were approaching a deep and wide gorge. The horses couldn't leap over the chasm, and a fall to the bottom would certainly mean death. Bridger turned his horse and faced the warrior. They both fired, and both horses were killed. Then they began a hand-to-hand battle with knives. The warrior was big and powerful. The two struggled and fought. One minute the warrior had the best of it; the next minute Bridger did. Until finally . . .

Here Bridger always paused, and one of his listeners would anxiously ask, "What happened?"

With a straight face, Bridger would reply, "Why, the Injun *killed* me!"

*   *   *

Jim Bridger was born in Richmond, Virginia, on March 17, 1804—the same year Lewis and Clark began their journey.

When he was eight years old, his family moved to St. Louis, where life was difficult. When Jim was twelve his mother died. Then his brother and father died, too. By the time Jim was fourteen, he and his little sister were the only survivors.

An aunt cared for his sister, but Jim had to find work. For a while he ran a flatboat, transporting wagons and livestock across the Mississippi River. Then Phil Creamer, a blacksmith in St. Louis, took Bridger as an apprentice.

A month before his eighteenth birthday, Bridger heard about William Ashley's ad in the newspaper. Bridger approached Major Henry, Ashley's partner, and became one of the young men chosen to go up the Missouri River.

Jim Bridger was barely eighteen years old when he left St. Louis to join the Ashley-Henry trapping expedition to the Rocky Mountains. He stayed in the West for most of the next sixty-seven years.

The keelboats left St. Louis on April 3, 1822, with Major Henry in command. On the way up the river, a band of Assiniboines pretended to be friendly, but suddenly stole about fifty horses as well as some supplies.

When the party arrived at the mouth of the Yellowstone River, they built Fort Henry and then began the fall hunt. The following April, a band of Blackfeet killed four of the trappers.

In early June, Jedediah Smith brought news that General Ashley's party had been attacked by the Arikaras on their way up the Missouri River. Fifteen of his men had been killed, and General Ashley needed Major Henry to come with reinforcements.

Bridger was one of twenty men Major Henry took downriver. Troops under Colonel Henry Leavenworth also responded from Fort Atkinson. From August 9–11, the mountain men and the army fought the Arikaras.

A treaty was signed in late August, and the party began the journey back to Fort Henry. Within days, they were attacked by Mandans. Bridger was uninjured, but two other trappers were killed.

Just weeks later, a grizzly bear almost killed a trapper named Hugh Glass. Of course, they couldn't bury Glass until he actually died. Since Major Henry's men needed to begin the fall hunt, Jim Bridger and John Fitzgerald stayed with Glass. As soon as he died, they would bury him and catch up with the party.

Days passed. Glass didn't die and didn't die. Bridger and Fitzgerald feared the Arikaras might find and kill them. Terrified, they decided to leave Glass alone assuming he would die anyway. They took his rifle, powder horn, bullet pouch, knife, and flint and gave them to Major Henry, saying that Glass had died. No one doubted their story, since it was obvious Glass had little chance to survive.

But Glass did not die. After Bridger and Fitzgerald left, he regained consciousness and crawled to a spring, where he rested and ate cherries and buffalo berries. Then he made his way three hundred fifty miles to Fort Kiowa. After regaining his strength, he wanted revenge, so he traveled a thousand miles more to Fort Henry.

When Glass arrived in February 1824, Bridger was astonished. Fitzgerald had left Fort Henry months earlier, but Bridger admitted his part in deserting Glass. Glass forgave Bridger, perhaps because Bridger was so young.

The following fall, Bridger was trapping with a party in Cache Valley, near today's Idaho-Utah border. One day a discussion began about where Bear River emptied. Bridger, the youngest member of the group, said he would find out. The other men laughed until he began building his bullboat.

Bridger floated down Bear River to where it emptied into a huge body of water. When he tasted the water, it was salty. He returned to camp and reported

This image, entitled *Jim Bridger in a Bull Boat*, illustrates Bridger's discovery of Great Salt Lake. Native Americans taught the mountain men how to build bullboats from willow branches or trunks, buffalo hide, and buffalo tallow. Bullboats look like large leather tubs, but they are practically unsinkable.

what he had found. The other trappers supposedly said, "Jim, you done found the Pacific Ocean!" It wasn't the Pacific Ocean, but Bridger is credited with being the first white man to discover Great Salt Lake.

In the summer of 1825, Bridger accompanied Ashley partway to St. Louis with the beaver pelts the trappers had brought to the first rendezvous. At Bighorn Canyon, near today's Wyoming-Montana line, the party had to decide whether to go through the canyon by water or land. The water route would be quicker, but was it safe?

While some of the men scouted the land route, Bridger built a log raft and went down the river by himself. The foaming river plunged down rapids and through narrow canyons, twisting and turning between one-thousand-foot-high rock walls. For Bridger to make the forty-mile trip alone on a wooden raft was incredible. Even the Native Americans admired his feat. They called the canyon Bad Pass. Bridger sent word back to Ashley *not* to risk taking the packs of furs down the river.

During that fall's hunt, Bridger trapped in what is today's Yellowstone National Park. He came back with stories of a river that ran so fast it was hot at the bottom (now called Firehole River), a forest of petrified trees, and a dark glass cliff (now called Obsidian Cliff). He told of geysers spouting water seventy feet in the air, and springs so hot that a person could cook his supper in them.

He described a place where the fish swam from the Atlantic Ocean to the Pacific Ocean and back again. Everyone laughed at his ridiculous story. But he wasn't kidding. Two Ocean Creek divides at Two Ocean Pass. One stream flows to the Snake River and eventually to the Pacific Ocean. The other stream flows to the Yellowstone River and eventually to the Atlantic Ocean. Fish swim from one stream to the other, actually swimming from the waters that become the Pacific to the waters that become the Atlantic. For years, Bridger's stories of these amazing spectacles were called "mountain man tales."

Bridger and four other mountain men—Thomas Fitzpatrick, Milton G. Sublette, Henry Fraeb, and Baptiste Gervais—bought out the fur company owned by Jedediah Smith, David E. Jackson, and William L. Sublette in July 1830. Bridger and his partners named it the Rocky Mountain Fur Company.

Jim Bridger first visited what is now Specimen Ridge, Fossil Forest, in Yellowstone National Park in 1826. The unknown man in the above photograph, taken by J. P. Iddings, is looking at the petrified trees about sixty-four years after Bridger first saw them.

In 1832, the summer rendezvous was in Pierre's Hole. The rendezvous was breaking up on July 18 when a battle broke out between 150 Gros Ventres of the Prairie and 700 trappers. The death toll was high. Accounts vary, but between 12 and 32 whites and friendly Native Americans were killed; between 10 and 26 Gros Ventres were killed.

The following October, Bridger and Tom Fitzpatrick's party met a band of over a hundred Blackfeet while they were trapping. The Blackfeet wanted to smoke the peace pipe. Cautiously, Tom Fitzpatrick took seven mountain men along to parley (which means "to have a discussion"), and the chief brought seven warriors. But some misunderstandings occurred and a battle began. Three mountain men and nine Blackfoot warriors were killed.

That evening, Bridger was back in camp lying on his stomach with two

In this picture, entitled *Going to the Rendezvous,* the group of mountain men who had been living and trapping together through the winter traveled to the rendezvous.

This painting by Frederic Remington is entitled *Trappers Going to Pierre's Hole Fight*. As the 1832 rendezvous in Pierre's Hole ended on July 18, a battle was fought between 700 trappers and 150 Gros Ventres of the Prairie.

arrows in his back. While Bridger bit down on a stick, Fitzpatrick cut into his back and freed the first arrow. But Tom could not remove the second arrow. Tom cut off the arrow shaft and told Bridger he would have to live with the arrow-head lodged in his back.

That arrow remained in Bridger's back until 1835, when Marcus Whitman attended the summer rendezvous. Whitman, a missionary and a surgeon, agreed to try to remove the arrow. The point had formed a hook when it struck the bone, and cartilage had grown around it. Dr. Whitman removed the arrowhead while everyone at the rendezvous watched with wonder and great astonishment.

Bridger felt so much better that he took a wife. Cora, his first wife, was the daughter of a Flathead chief.

In 1839, Jim Bridger returned to St. Louis—his first visit in seventeen years. He was used to wearing buckskin clothes, so store-bought clothes felt odd. He was also used to sleeping on the ground. A bed with a mattress was so uncomfort-

Sir William Drummond Stewart, a wealthy Scottish nobleman, had attended the 1830 and 1833 rendezvous. When he returned to the rendezvous in 1837, he brought Bridger a gift—a full suit of armor. Alfred Jacob Miller, a portrait painter who was traveling with Sir William, painted the above picture of Bridger.

When Jim Bridger and Louis Vasquez built Fort Bridger in 1843, there was no other fort between Fort Laramie and Fort Hall. Bridger stocked the fort with goods and built a blacksmith shop where he repaired anything from guns to wagons. This image is a detail from a drawing in the Wyoming State Archives.

able that he borrowed a buffalo hide and slept on the floor. However, he enjoyed eating bread, which he had not tasted since he left St. Louis.

Bridger and Louis Vasquez became partners, and in 1843 they built Fort Bridger on the Black Fork of the Green River in today's Wyoming. Fort Bridger was almost in the middle of the 620-mile trail between Fort Laramie and Fort Hall. It was an important layover station for wagons going to Oregon or California, including the Donner party in 1846.

Jim Bridger's experience in the mountains and his knowledge of the West made him one of the area's most reliable guides. In the summer of 1849, he guided Captain Howard Stansbury's Corps of Topographical Engineers through the Wasatch Mountains to Great Salt Lake.

A year later, Captain Stansbury asked Bridger if he could find a direct route between Fort Bridger and the South Platte River. Bridger didn't have to "find" the route. He already knew the country. Using a stick, he drew a map in the dirt. He then guided Captain Stansbury over the trail. This route between the mountains became known as Bridger's Pass. It was later used by the Overland Stage Company, the Pony Express, and the Union Pacific Railroad.

Captain Stansbury's report included a September 1850 meeting with a group of Sioux and Cheyenne. The two tribes did not speak the same language, but Bridger talked to the group for over an hour using sign language. Both tribes

This drawing of Jim Bridger is by Frederic Remington. Even though Bridger could not read or write, he could make a better and more accurate map than the government men with their scientific equipment.

shared surprise, interest, and laughter and obviously understood what Bridger was "saying," although he never spoke a word.

In September 1851, a great peace council was held near Fort Laramie to map the boundaries of each tribe's hunting grounds. The army also wanted an agreement that they could establish posts and build roads. Almost three hundred army troops and ten thousand Native Americans attended. Jim Bridger served as interpreter for the Shoshones, since he could speak English, Spanish, and (frontier) French, plus the languages of a dozen of the tribes—including Bannock, Crow, Snake, Pend d'Oreille, Flathead, Nez Percé, and Ute.

All the chiefs had differing opinions, all wanted to be heard, and all made very long speeches. It took time, patience, and diplomacy to interpret and negotiate with the tribes, many of whom were bitter enemies. The council successfully established boundaries, but the peace lasted only three years.

Bridger met Brigham Young on the trail in 1847 when Young was leading the Latter-day Saints (commonly known as the Mormons) to the West to avoid religious persecution. Friction arose at that meeting, and the bitterness between Bridger and the Mormons grew over the years. The Mormons accused Bridger of providing arms and ammunition to the Native Americans and retaliated by attacking his fort in 1853. Bridger escaped and took his family to Missouri. The Mormons took control of Fort Bridger, but the army made it a military base in 1858. It was also used as a Pony Express station in 1860–1861.

Bridger had an extraordinary sense of the wilderness. After exploring a region once, he never forgot its geography. As Major General Grenville M. Dodge said, "The whole West was mapped out in his mind," and "he could smell his way where he could not see it."

Colonel Albert Sidney Johnston hired Bridger to guide the new governor of Utah Territory, Alfred Cumming, and his staff to Utah in 1857. The party consisted of 2,500 army troops, 312 wagons, 3,250 oxen, and 360 civilians. Brigham Young issued a "Proclamation of War" to stop the invasion, but no shots were fired. In the spring of 1858, Bridger successfully guided the governor's party to Salt Lake City. Colonel Johnston gave Bridger the honorary title of major, and he was often referred to as Major Bridger the rest of his life.

From 1859 to 1860, Bridger guided Captain William F. Raynolds' Corps of Topographical Engineers to the Yellowstone River area to determine routes for roads. Despite terrible weather, Raynolds made what was the accepted map of the region for many years, and he credited Bridger's knowledge of the country.

The next year, Bridger served as guide for Captain E. L. Berthoud, chief engineer for the Overland Stage Company, to plot the shortest stagecoach route between Denver and Salt Lake City. Today it is U.S. Route 40, which goes over Berthoud Pass.

In October 1863, Bridger guided Captain J. Lee Humfreville in the South Park of Colorado. Over the following winter, they shared quarters at Fort Laramie. Bridger often slept in the afternoon, then awoke at midnight to roast meat, eat, sing Native American songs, and beat on a tin pan like a tom-tom.

Since Captain Humfreville followed a military schedule, he needed his sleep. He thought reading to Bridger might keep him awake during the day, so he read him *Hiawatha* by Henry Wadsworth Longfellow. But Bridger disagreed with Longfellow, saying, "No such Injun ever lived" and that the story was "infernal lies."

Bridger asked Humfreville which was the best book ever written. Humfreville said it was Shakespeare's works. As the plays were read aloud, Bridger memorized various passages. But when he repeated them later, they included mountain man jargon!

A legend says that Bridger once stopped a wagon train and traded a yoke of oxen worth $125 for a book of Shakespeare's plays, and paid a German boy $40 a month to read to him.

In 1865, the Cheyenne, Sioux, and Arapaho were raiding small communities and attacking stagecoaches and wagon trains in the Powder River region in present-day Wyoming. Bridger went to work for the army as a guide.

On August 26, Bridger told Captain H. E. Palmer and General Patrick Edward Connor that he saw a column of smoke over a ridge fifty miles away—a sign Native Americans were there. Bridger was not using field glasses, so both officers peered through theirs. They didn't see smoke and declared there was none.

Bridger was indignant. He rode away with some men and made a remark about the "paper-collar soldiers." Bridger *had* seen smoke. When the scouts returned, they reported an Arapaho tribe.

Three days later, the troops fought the Battle of Tongue River, killing a chief and 63 warriors. They captured 1,100 horses, burned 250 lodges, and destroyed the meat the Arapaho were drying for the coming winter. The surviving men, women, and children, were left with no meat, no horses, and no shelter. This was the last battle sixty-one-year-old Bridger ever fought.

In 1867, Colonel Henry B. Carrington hired Bridger to guide an expedition that built three forts and measured distances along the 967-mile Bozeman Trail from Fort Kearny, Nebraska, to Virginia City, Montana. Before the expedition began, the army tried to cut costs by discharging Jim Bridger. But the colonel insisted on using Bridger because he knew the country so well. Bridger remained as the guide.

Bridger also assisted Major General Grenville M. Dodge in surveying the Union Pacific Railroad.

Bridger's personal life was filled with tragedy. His first wife died in the winter of 1845–1846. They had three children. Their oldest daughter, Mary Ann, was killed the next year when a band of Cayuse attacked Dr. Marcus Whitman's mission, where she attended school.

Bridger married his second wife, a Ute, in 1848. She died on July 4, 1849, while giving birth to a daughter whom Bridger named Virginia Rosalie. There is a story that he killed a buffalo cow every few days and fed his baby daughter the buffalo's milk.

In 1850, Bridger married his third wife, Little Fawn. She was the daughter of Chief Washakie, a Snake (Shoshone). Little Fawn died in 1858.

When Bridger was sixty-seven years old, his health was deteriorating and his eyesight was failing. He went to Missouri in the spring of 1871 and lived with his daughter Virginia.

Ten years later Bridger died on July 17, 1881.

JEDEDIAH STRONG SMITH (1799-1831)

Mountain Man, Fur Trapper and Trader, Explorer, Discoverer of South Pass for Westbound Emigrants, First White Man to Cross the Sierra Nevada, First White Man to Cross the Great Basin, First White Man to Explore the California-Oregon Coast by Land

While Jim Bridger was a typical mountain man, Jedediah Smith was probably the most unusual. He was smart *and* literate. He wrote letters and kept a journal during the eight years he was in the West. He also made accurate maps of the wilderness he crossed.

Raised a strict Methodist, Smith was very religious and always carried and read his Bible. He was devoted to his family, and sent money home to help his parents. In his will, he left all of his money to his family.

For the times, he was quite well-off. Unlike most mountain men, he did not spend his money wildly at the rendezvous. Smith was usually clean-shaven, did not drink, never used tobacco, and was not romantic with women.

Jedediah Strong Smith was born on January 6, 1799, in the village of Jericho (now called Bainbridge) in Chenango County, New York. He was the sixth of fourteen children.

In 1811, his family moved to Erie County, Pennsylvania, where the local doctor tutored young Jedediah. Dr. Titus Gordon Vespasian Simons taught him reading, writing, Latin, and English. Dr. Simons gave him a copy of Meriwether Lewis and William Clark's book of their journey to the Pacific Ocean.

Eleven years later General William H. Ashley hired Smith as one of the one hundred "enterprising young men" to accompany Major Henry to the Rocky Mountains.

The following May, Major Henry sent Smith to meet Ashley's supply boats. Major Henry wanted Ashley to buy horses at the Arikara villages, since the Assiniboines had stolen many of Henry's horses over the winter.

This image of Jedidah Smith was made by a friend after Smith's death. After a bear attack in the fall of 1823, Smith wore his hair long to hide the scars and missing eyebrow. Smith was probably the most outstanding of the mountain men.

Smith joined Ashley's ninety men on May 29, but Ashley found trading with the Arikaras to be difficult. The Arikaras demanded guns and powder. When Ashley refused, the trading ceased.

In the middle of the night, an Arikara killed Aaron Stephens. The next morning, a battle began with 700 Arikara warriors. By the time Ashley's men withdrew, 11 trappers had been injured and 15 killed.

Ashley needed reinforcements from Major Henry, so Smith and another man volunteered to return to Fort Henry. They arrived in the middle of June. Smith, Major Henry, and about twenty of his men then joined General Ashley the first week of July.

Colonel Henry Leavenworth at Fort Atkinson, in present-day Nebraska, also responded, bringing six companies of soldiers. The troops and the mountain men battled the Arikaras from August 9–11. A treaty was finally negotiated at the end of August.

First Expedition: 1823-1826

That fall, Ashley gave Smith command of a party of trappers. Days later in the Black Hills of South Dakota, a grizzly bear grabbed Smith by the head, threw him to the ground, and ripped the top of his head open from his left eye to his right ear.

The other trappers killed the bear, but they didn't know what to do for Smith. Each claimed he didn't have any "surgical knowledge." Smith was still conscious, so he sent two men for water, and he told Jim Clyman to get out a needle and thread and sew his head back together.

Clyman stitched the skin back in place, but when he was almost finished, Smith's ear still dangled—held only by a piece of flesh. Clyman said he couldn't

Jedediah Smith was aboard the second keelboat General Ashley sent up the Missouri River headed for the Rocky Mountains. The boat, much like the one shown above, left St. Louis on May 8, 1822. About three weeks later, a mast caught in a tree limb and the boat sank, along with $10,000 worth of cargo. As soon as Ashley heard about the accident, he equipped another boat, and within a few weeks, the party was under way again.

This image, entitled *Attack on the Ashley Party*, illustrates the 1823 battle between Ashley's men and the Arikaras. This battle, in which fifteen of Smith's fellow trappers were killed, has been called the beginning of the Indian Wars of the West.

do anything with the ear. Smith said, "O you must try to stick [it] up some way or other."

Clyman did the best he could. After he finished stitching Smith's head, they rode a mile to where there was water. The men set up camp and cared for Smith. After ten days, they resumed their journey, heading for the mountains to begin trapping.

Smith and about a dozen other men spent the 1823–1824 winter with a party of Crow people. The Crow indicated there were lots of beaver in the valley of the Seedskeedee, which is now called the Green River. The Crow drew a map on the back of a deer hide.

Using those directions, Smith and his party discovered South Pass at the end of February 1824. South Pass was a low pass where travelers with wagons could cross the Continental Divide. It had been used by Native Americans for centuries and had been crossed in 1812 by a party of white men going east led by Robert Stuart, but it did not appear on maps or become known until Smith's party discovered it. It became part of the Oregon Trail.

A year later, in the summer of 1825, Ashley held the first trappers' rendezvous on Henry's Fork. Major Henry retired from the fur trade that fall, and Ashley made Jedediah Smith a partner as well as a field captain.

At the 1826 rendezvous, Jedediah Smith, David E. Jackson, and William L. Sublette bought Ashley's fur business. That fall, Jackson and Sublette took trapping parties north into familiar areas, while Smith took a party south and west into unexplored country.

This painting of a grizzly bear was done by Alfred Jacob Miller. An average adult grizzly bear weighs about eight hundred pounds and stands eight feet high on its hind legs. It has razor-sharp claws, a ferocious bite, and can kill a man with a single blow.

Members of the Crow nation drew a map for Jedediah Smith to show him a route to the Green River in Wyoming. Smith realized it was a pass over the Continental Divide, later called South Pass, which had a slope so gradual Smith knew wagons would be able to cross these imposing ranges.

Second Expedition: 1826–1827

Smith's expedition of seventeen men left the rendezvous on August 16, 1826. By mid-September, the men were suffering. The weather was hot. The hilly terrain was rocky and dusty. Game was scarce, and they had eaten all their dried buffalo meat.

One afternoon, Smith's expedition encountered a group of Paiutes. Although extremely poor, they shared their corn and pumpkins, which were a real feast for the hungry men.

The party followed the Virgin River. With nothing to graze on, half of the horses died. Those still alive were too weak to carry their packs. The men, too, were half-starved, and their only water had been from the muddy river. Luckily, a tribe of Mojaves took them to their village and gave them food.

They stayed with the tribe for two weeks, resting and trading for horses. One of the Mojaves spoke some Spanish, as did Abraham Laplant, so Smith

This photograph was taken fifty years after Jedediah Smith traveled along the Virgin River, but the terrain had not changed since Smith's expedition. The picture, taken by J. K. Hillers, shows how rocky the terrain was and how difficult it was for the horses to traverse the country.

It took Jedediah Smith and his men about two weeks to cross the Mojave Desert in 1826. Their food supply was low and they often went for days without water. The above illustration of Smith's crossing of the Mojave was painted by Frederic Remington.

learned about the desert they were about to cross. Two Native Americans who had escaped from a California mission were living with the Mojaves and agreed to guide Smith.

The party left on November 10, following the Mojave River. Smith called it the Inconstant River since it flowed for a while, disappeared into the sand, and then reappeared. It took them fifteen days to cross the Mojave Desert.

They went through the San Bernardino Mountains and arrived at the San Gabriel Mission, near present-day Los Angeles, on November 26. Exhausted and ragged, they were the first European Americans to travel to California overland through the desert.

The head of the mission, Father Jose Bernardo Sanchez, offered them hospitality, including plenty of food. Since the men's clothing was ragged, he provided sixty-four yards of fabric so that each man could make a new shirt.

California was part of Mexico, so Smith wrote a letter to request permission to travel through the country. Two weeks later, an order arrived for Smith to meet with the governor in San Diego. Smith told Governor Jose Maria Echeandia that he and his men were beaver trappers, that they had come to California over the desert, and that they wanted to go north to return to the Rocky Mountains.

The governor was suspicious. He did not understand what beaver trapping was or why these men would want to do this. Why would men come so far looking for small animals? The governor's lack of understanding seems surprising, since the sea otter trade had been going on for almost forty years on the northwest coast just north of California.

Over the next four days, Governor Echeandia questioned Smith three times. He knew of no Spanish word to describe what Smith and his men did. Since they trapped the beaver in streams and rivers, Echeandia called Smith a *pescador*—a fisherman.

The governor didn't know how to handle the situation. His superiors in Mexico City would be angry if he let Smith's party go. If he put them in jail, he feared trouble with the American government, since Smith had passports, a license, and papers from General Ashley. Echeandia decided to wait for instructions from Mexico City. Meanwhile, Jedediah Smith waited and waited.

The solution to the problem came unexpectedly. Six American ships were in port in San Diego Harbor. On December 20, the shipmasters gave the governor a petition vouching for Smith and his men. During the first week of January 1827, the governor released Smith on the condition that his party leave by the same route they used to enter California.

Smith returned to the mission on January 10, and the party left San Gabriel a week later. Following Governor Echeandia's orders, Smith left through the San Bernardino Mountains. But once they were out of the California settlements, Smith felt he was no longer under the governor's authority. Instead of retracing their route over the Mojave Desert, Smith turned north. He and his men came to trap beaver, and that was what they intended to do.

By the end of April, they had reached the American River and had accumulated 1,500 pounds of beaver pelts. The first week of May they tried to cross the Sierra Nevada, but the freezing temperatures and deep snow stopped them. Six of their horses died. They returned to the Stanislaus River and made a camp where most of the party could wait.

On May 20, Smith, Silas Gobel, and Robert Evans took seven horses and two mules to try to cross the Sierra Nevada again. By May 24, they were in four feet of snow. The next day the snow was eight feet deep. That night a violent storm raged, and the next day, two horses and one mule froze to death before their eyes.

On May 27 the weather cleared, so they started their journey again. Eight days later, they were over the Sierra Nevada.

Then they faced the desert and the unbearable heat. Their horses grew weaker each day. They saw a few Native Americans at a distance and approached a campfire where a Paiute woman was cooking scorpions for supper. She and her two small children were terrified, but shared their water with the men.

When one of their horses died on June 16, they ate it to keep from starving. Two days later, a group of Paiutes led them to a spring, shared two small ground squirrels, and pointed out an edible plant. Three days later, another horse got into a mire and the men had to kill it. Once again they ate horse meat.

Their situation became desperate by June 24. Late that afternoon, they dug holes and buried themselves in the sand to escape the heat. After resting, they traveled all night. They had no water that day. Smith wrote that he was afraid they would "perish in the desert unheard of and unpitied." He wished to be back home with his family.

The next morning, Robert Evans could go no farther. He lay down beside a small cedar to die. Smith and Gobel were too weak to help him. If they stayed with him, all three would die. So the two went on.

Amazingly, within three miles, they found a spring. They drank their fill and Gobel threw himself into the water. Smith filled a kettle with water and returned to Evans, who was so weak he was almost dead.

Smith helped Evans drink an entire gallon of water, Evans then asked Smith, "Why didn't you bring more?"

Evans revived and was able to walk to the spring. The men spent that day resting, then continued across the desert. They arrived at the rendezvous on July 3. Only one horse and one mule survived.

Third Expedition: 1827-1829

Ten days later, Smith again departed for California, to regroup with the men he had left behind. Eighteen men went along, including Silas Gobel. The party followed Smith's route of the previous year. Again they met the Mojaves. Smith traded for horses, wheat, beans, dried pumpkin, melons, and corn. He did not know that some other trappers had killed many Mojaves recently, and that they had become leary of whites.

On August 18, Smith's party began ferrying their gear on a raft across the Colorado River. Smith and half the men crossed the river. The other group waited with the horses on the east bank until the rafts could return to carry the remaining gear across.

Suddenly, without warning, the Mojaves attacked the men on the east bank. The trappers were totally defenseless, and the warriors killed ten men, including Silas Gobel. They captured two Native American women who were traveling with the party. Although they beat Thomas Virgin on the head, he managed to cross the river to join Smith.

Smith's party had five guns, a little ammunition, fifteen pounds of meat, and their butcher knives. They had no horses and had to leave behind the bodies of their friends. They were about a half mile down river when almost five hundred warriors closed around them.

The nine men took cover in a cluster of small cottonwood trees. They made lances by attaching their butcher knives to the ends of tree branches. The men asked Smith if he thought they could defend themselves. Smith told them he thought they could, but in his journal he wrote that was not his true opinion.

For a while, the warriors kept their distance. When a few approached, Smith ordered his two best riflemen to fire. They killed two Mojaves and injured another. The warriors retreated and didn't pursue them again. Smith called it "a fearful time."

When it was almost dark, the group started across the 150-mile desert, trying to care for Thomas Virgin's severe head injuries. They traveled all night. The next morning, they found a spring and stayed there through the heat of the day.

Traveling by night and resting by day, it took them almost ten days to cross the desert. Luckily they found springs, and a group of Paiutes provided some horses and food. They also obtained two more horses from some Serrano people.

Once in California, they went north to where Smith had left his first party in 1826. The reunion was joyous until the men learned of the massacre.

A few days later, Smith and three of his men went to the San Jose Mission. Smith had been welcomed at the San Gabriel Mission in 1826, so he was surprised when the priests at San Jose treated his party as spies and intruders.

Smith wrote to the governor and, two weeks later, soldiers arrived and took him to San Diego. Governor Echeandia was not happy that Smith had returned to California. Again he could not decide what to do with the men. Weeks passed and Echeandia made no decision. Then on November 7, four American sea captains, whose ships were in port in Monterey, agreed to act as agents to insure that Smith and his men would leave California.

Within days, Smith was released. Taking 315 horses and mules, Smith's party was back in the wilderness on December 30. Smith planned to sell the horses at the rendezvous.

About four weeks later, two men deserted the expedition, taking eleven traps with them. This was a serious problem, since they had already lost so much of their equipment to the Mojaves.

As the party traveled north through California, they looked for a pass through the Sierra Nevada. There were beaver and lots of game, so the men had plenty to eat, and the Native Americans they met were peaceful. But thick vegetation, rain, marshes, flooded rivers, mud, and bears made traveling difficult.

On March 9, Harrison Rogers was severely bitten by a bear. Smith dressed Rogers' wounds with plasters of cold water and a salve made from sugar and soap. Rogers could not travel for a week.

A month later, Smith escaped one bear by jumping "head foremost" into a creek. A short time after that, another bear charged Smith and the horse he was riding. The terrified horse took off running, but the bear caught the horse's tail and hung on. The horse dragged the bear quite a distance before it finally let loose. Smith wrote that he and his horse were both glad to be rid of the bear's company.

As the party continued north, Smith finally gave up on finding a pass through the Sierra Nevada. Instead he headed northwest. But the difficulties made it almost impossible.

One mountain was so rocky, it took four hours to travel one mile. They negotiated their way through thick, tangled brush and dense fog, and around enormous boulders. They were blocked by sharp cliffs, deep ravines, steep embankments, thick timber, and fast-running streams. In such difficult terrain, there was no game, and the men were cold, hungry, exhausted, and discouraged.

Day after day, week after week, conditions kept getting worse. The horses' hooves were mangled from the rocks, and they kept falling from exhaustion. To make matters worse, keeping track of over three hundred horses was difficult. Every evening several men would backtrack to find strays. On April 15, a band of Wintun wounded some of the men and killed some of the horses.

With no game, the men killed their dog on June 5, and on June 6 they killed one of their horses. Three days later, Smith went hunting by himself and managed to kill three elk. When he took the meat back to camp, the "moody silence of hunger" was replaced with cooking, feasting, and joy.

A couple of weeks later, there was more game, but also more obstacles. The Native Americans had dug ten-foot pits to trap elk. Unfortunately, many of Smith's horses fell into the camouflaged pits. The men labored to get them out.

It seemed the journey could get no worse, but it did. Some of the mules carrying packs fell over precipices. Near the end of June, 23 horses and mules died in various accidents in a span of three days. Many animals were so exhausted or badly injured that they had to be abandoned.

On July 3, a band of Native Americans ran away from them and left behind a ten-year-old Native American boy. The men fed him and named him Marion. He had been taken from his family in the Willamette Valley and made a slave. He was glad to go with the white men. The expedition continued north to the Umpqua River in present-day Oregon.

On July 13, they camped near a small tributary, and a tribe of Kelawatset came to their camp and traded beaver and otter skins, eels, and elk meat. The next morning a Kelawatset guide took Smith, John Turner, and Richard Leland in his canoe to determine the best place to get the horses across the river. As they returned to the bank near the camp, there was no sign of Smith's men. That seemed strange.

Then a warrior on shore said something, and Smith's guide suddenly overturned the canoe, dumping Smith and his men into the water. Native Americans hiding in the bushes began firing as the men scrambled for shore. Smith knew something terrible had happened since none of his men came to investigate when the gunfire started.

Smith, Turner, and Leland narrowly escaped. Their only hope was to get help at Fort Vancouver, one hundred miles away.

They didn't know it, but one other member of their party was also heading for Fort Vancouver. That morning, two warriors had attacked Arthur Black with tomahawks while two hundred others massacred the rest of the party. Black, a large and powerful man, was able to overthrow his attackers and escape.

Black headed north, but another group of Native Americans robbed him of his clothes and knife. Later a band of friendly Tillamooks guided him to Fort Vancouver. Black arrived on August 8. Dr. John McLoughlin was in charge of the fort. Although he worked for the rival Hudson's Bay Company, he offered kindness and hospitality to Black. Black thought he was the only survivor, but two days later, Smith, Turner, and Leland arrived at Fort Vancouver.

McLoughlin sent a party to help Smith recover as much of his outfit as possible. Despite terrible rains, they recovered approximately seven hundred beaver skins, which Smith sold to McLoughlin; less than forty horses and mules; some of their equipment; and portions of Smith's and Harrison Rogers' journals. When they reached the massacre site, Smith buried the remains of his friends.

After spending the winter at Fort Vancouver, Smith and Arthur Black left in March to return to the Rocky Mountains. They met up with David Jackson and William Sublette, Smith's partners, but the reunion was saddened by the two massacres. The twenty-four deaths were the worst disaster in the history of the fur trade.

This picture by William Henry Jackson shows the wagon train of supplies leaving
St. Louis in April 1830, the last year Smith and his partners, David Jackson and William Sublette,
supplied the rendezvous. They sold their company to Jim Bridger and his partners that summer.

At the 1830 summer rendezvous, Smith, Jackson, and Sublette sold their fur company to Jim Bridger and his four partners. In August, Smith returned to St. Louis.

The next spring, the Mexican government was welcoming American traders, so Smith and two of his brothers headed for Santa Fe with wagons of trade goods. Near present-day Dodge City, Kansas, the caravan left the Arkansas River and went south to find the Cimarron River. After three days, the men were in desperate need of water, and some of the animals were collapsing.

On May 27, Smith went ahead to find water. Seeing a damp spot, he bent down and dug a hole. Slowly water rose in the hole, but at the same time a Comanche hunting party surrounded him, and one man shot Smith in the shoulder. Smith killed the chief, but the other warriors killed Smith.

The details of Smith's death were learned when some Mexican traders brought his guns to Santa Fe. The traders said they got the guns from a band of Comanches who told them what had happened.

Jedediah Smith's accomplishments were remarkable. He was the first white man to cross South Pass westbound and the first to tell of its accessibility as an easy route across the Continental Divide.

Smith was the first European American to enter California by the overland route, the first to cross the Sierra Nevada, and the first to cross the Great Basin. He was the first white man to cross Nevada, the first to cross Utah from north to south, and the first to cross Utah from west to east.

He was also the first white man to travel from California to the Columbia River by land, and the first to draw a map showing the geography of the Rocky Mountains and the Great Basin.

Jedediah Smith survived the three worst battles between trappers and Native American tribes in the history of the American fur trade: the 1823 battle with the Arikaras, the 1827 Mojave massacre, and the 1828 Umpqua massacre.

Smith was thirty-two years old when he died on May 27, 1831. He had no wife and no children. He was one of America's greatest explorers.

JOSEPH REDDEFORD WALKER (1798-1876)

Mountain Man, Fur Trapper, Explorer, Trail Blazer, First White Man to Visit Yosemite, First White Man to See the Giant Redwood Trees, First to Travel the California Trail, First White Man to Take an Expedition Across the Sierra Nevada from East to West, Discoverer of Walker Pass, Guide for Emigrants and the U.S. Army

Joseph Walker rarely returned to Missouri, so when he visited in 1836, his extended family gathered to see their famous frontier hero relative—Captain Walker.

Everyone knew Joseph Walker spent a lot of his time with the native peoples and that his wife was a member of the Snake, or Shoshone, tribe. But few understood why he would choose such a rugged lifestyle.

Joseph Reddeford Walker was handsome, stood over six feet tall, and weighed more than two hundred pounds. He was a powerful man, brave but also brilliant. He led his men on a difficult and dangerous expedition to California in 1833, and he brought them home alive—there were no fatalities. Alfred Jacob Miller painted this portrait of Walker after the California expedition.

A cousin from Alabama asked if he had had enough of the wilderness and was returning to civilization to become a settled citizen.

Joseph Walker replied that he wasn't. He said, "[I'm going back] to live with the Indians because white people are too damn mean."

Joseph Walker was born on December 13, 1798, in Roane County, Tennessee. With three brothers and three sisters, he grew up learning how to use weapons, hunt, butcher game, tan hides, cook, sew, do basic carpentry, and handle horses, cattle, and hogs.

Because he could read and write, he was considered educated. But since he didn't keep a journal and never bragged about his accomplishments, the story of his travels has been collected from others' journals and their memories. If he had not been such a private man, he might have been remembered as one of the greatest explorers and leaders of the West.

When he was twenty-one, Walker joined a trapping expedition to Santa Fe. The Spanish imprisoned the men as intruders, but soon released them so that they could help fight the Pawnees.

In the summer of 1822, Walker and some companions were in the desert between the Arkansas and Cimarron rivers east of Santa Fe. They saw a group of men who were obviously in need of water. When they approached, Joseph was amazed to see his brother Joel. The brothers had not seen each other for over a year, and it was an unbelievable coincidence to meet in the middle of a desert hundreds of miles from civilization.

Joel later wrote that his party was alarmed when they saw what they thought was a band of warriors riding toward them. Thirsty and too weak to fight, they assumed they would be massacred. He wrote, "I kept my eyes on them and saw as I supposed, an Indian with his hair flying up and down. He came up and to my immense astonishment I saw he was my brother, Capt. Joe Walker."

Over the next five years, Joseph Walker raised livestock in Missouri, surveyed part of the Santa Fe Trail, and became the first sheriff of Jackson County.

In 1831, Walker met Captain Benjamin Bonneville, who was organizing a trapping expedition to the Rocky Mountains. Walker joined the party. They left Missouri on May 1, 1832, and reached the Green River on July 27.

After a year, Bonneville divided the men into three groups. One group returned to St. Louis to sell their furs, the second went toward Oregon to trap, and the third went with Joseph Walker to California. Walker was to search for new trapping country, find a trade route to the Pacific Ocean, and gather information on California's geography, military strength, natural resources, and people.

First Expedition: 1833–1834

At the 1833 rendezvous, over sixty men joined Walker. He hired twenty-four-year-old Zenas Leonard as the clerk and second in command. Leonard's journal is the record of the expedition. He obviously respected Walker, as he wrote, "Mr. Walker was a man well calculated to undertake a business of this kind. He was well hardened to the hardships of the wilderness—understood the character of the Indians very well—was kind and affable to his men, but at the same time at liberty to command without giving offence—and to explore unknown regions was his chief delight."

Each man took four horses, and the party left on July 24. They crossed the desert west of Great Salt Lake and followed a river Walker called the Barren River, today's Humboldt. Around October 1, they were in the Humboldt Sink in today's western Nevada when they encountered hundreds of Paiutes. Extremely poor, these people lived in huts made of sagebrush. They ate seeds, bulbs, roots of desert plants, grasshoppers, lizards, crickets, dried ants, and the grubs of flies.

The white men's equipment fascinated the Paiutes, and they stole tools, knives, beaver traps, and horses. Walker warned his men not to kill the Paiutes, but the thievery infuriated the trappers and they killed four of them. Walker reprimanded them, but it was too late.

The Paiutes sang their death chants, then between five hundred and nine hundred warriors swarmed around Walker's men. The Paiutes had never seen rifles and they laughed at the trappers' threats. The men fired at some ducks on a nearby lake. The noise of the rifles frightened the warriors, and they fell flat on the ground. Walker and his men had thwarted the attack.

In the summer of 1833, in western Nevada, Walker's party was in desert country, much like the above illustration. They camped in an area called the Humboldt Sink, which is a region of marshes, bogs, and shallow lakes. It is called a sink because the waters in this area sink into the sand and disappear, having no sea in which to drain.

The next morning, as Walker's party moved through the Humboldt Sink, huge numbers of Paiutes tried to set up an ambush. One trapper estimated there were twelve hundred of them. When about four hundred began to advance, Walker gave orders to fire. The trappers killed thirty-nine warriors before the Paiutes withdrew.

Walker received criticism for this incident, but both George Nidever's and Zenas Leonard's journals claim the small group of trappers were about to be massacred and the attack was necessary to save their lives. Furthermore, the two massacres of Jedediah Smith's men were still fresh on the mountain men's minds.

By the time Walker's party reached the Sierra Nevada, there was no game and they were running out of food. One evening, the hunters discovered an abandoned shelter. Inside were rabbit-skin bags containing what looked like dried fish. The hunters took the bags back to camp and dumped the contents into the stew cooking over the fire. The men ate the stew for supper and had the leftovers the next morning.

At breakfast, Walker discovered the "dried fish" in the stew was *not* dried fish at all. It was insect larvae—worms!

Not one man finished his breakfast.

The expedition entered the mountains in October, near what is now called the Walker River. The terrain was terrible, with huge boulders, rock-walled canyons, and deep snow in the gullies and crevasses. The men were constantly threatened by rock slides and avalanches.

The men dug a trail through the snow and moved rocks, brush, and fallen trees so that the horses could get through. There was still no game, and the men were hungry. Some of them wanted to turn back. With nothing to graze on, most of the horses were about to die, so Walker allowed the men to kill two horses and eat the tough, stringy meat. Over the following weeks, they ate seventeen of their horses as the animals sank to the ground from starvation.

After three weeks of cold, exhaustion, discouragement, and hunger, Walker and his men came out of the mountains. They were the first white men to cross the Sierra Nevada from east to west. Once again they found plenty of game and plenty for the surviving horses to graze on.

On October 20 the party reached the rim of a cliff that was almost straight up and down. Below them lay a beautiful valley. But to descend to the bottom, they had to lower the horses, their gear, and themselves by using ropes.

Walker and his party had discovered Yosemite Valley. The sight was so spectacular that many of Walker's men considered seeing the valley one of the highlights of their lives. Joseph Walker was so proud of the discovery that he had the words "Camped in Yosemite, November 13, 1833" inscribed on his gravestone.

Just days later, Walker's party made another discovery: the giant redwood trees, the *Sequoia gigantea.*

On November 20 they reached the Pacific Ocean, which Leonard called "the extreme end of the great west." They were amazed at the size of a carcass of a ninety-foot whale that they found on the beach.

While camped near the ocean, the men spotted the sails of a ship off the coast, and they hoisted a makeshift white flag. The ship approached and some of the crew came ashore. It was the *Lagoda,* an American ship out of Boston. The ship's crew and the mountain men celebrated together. The *Lagoda's* captain,

This engraving, entitled *Descent into the Valley*, illustrates the difficult terrain Walker's party negotiated in the mountains above the Yosemite Valley.

John Bradshaw, provided delicacies such as cheese and bread for the mountain men. On shore, the mountain men cooked fresh meat for the sailors.

Bonneville had obtained passports and Mexican visas for Walker's party. Governor Jose Figueroa welcomed Walker and his men and gave them permission to spend the winter in California. Six of Walker's men chose to remain there.

The rest of Walker's party began their return journey on February 14, 1834, taking 340 horses, 47 head of cattle, and 30 dogs, which were to be used as food. With two Tubatulabel men as guides, they took a southern route to cross the Sierra Nevada. The pass they used was later named Walker Pass.

Yosemite has been called the most beautiful place on earth, and Joseph Walker and his men were the first white men to see it. The picture above, entitled *General View of the Great Yo-Semite Valley*, was painted by Thomas A. Ayres in 1849, sixteen years after Walker and his men had visited.

This photograph was taken by E. C. Watkins twenty-five years after Walker's party first saw the big trees. It is believed to be the first photograph ever made of a *Sequoia gigantea*.

Once on the east side of the mountains, they intended to travel north through Owens Valley until they found their trail from the previous fall. But there was little grass for the livestock and the animals were growing weaker. The men were discouraged, so Walker decided to take a shortcut northeast across the present-day Nevada desert.

They knew the crossing would be difficult, but the situation soon became desperate. There was no water and no grass. The wind blew thick dust clouds that blinded both the animals and the men. The heat and the dust parched their throats, and the rock and sand bruised and cut the livestock's hooves.

Half of their dogs died. Then the larger animals began dying as well. The men were so thirsty that they drained the blood of the dead animals and drank it. They used the hides of the dead cattle to make moccasins for the animals that were still alive.

After two days, men and animals were scattered in every direction for over a mile. Walker ordered a halt to get the entire expedition back together. Leonard wrote that they "presented a really forlorn spectacle."

At midnight they decided to return to the valley. They traveled all night without stopping. They had to keep the livestock moving because if an

While Joseph Walker's party spent the 1833–1834 winter in California, the men were amazed at some of the Spanish men's entertainment. One event Zenas Leonard called bull-baiting involved lassoing bulls and bears, as in the illustration above. The men placed bets and then turned the bears and bulls loose to fight.

Walker spent the winter of 1833–1834 in California and then took a southern route to cross the Sierra Nevada. With a pack train looking similar to the one in the above illustration, his party used a pass that was later named Walker Pass.

animal lay down, it would refuse to get up again, and they would have to leave it to die.

The next day, the horses suddenly became unmanageable. The men let them lead, knowing that they had caught the scent of water. Nearby was grass for the livestock and wood to build a fire.

A few days later, they found the trail they had made on their way to California.

When the expedition arrived at the Bear River in July, they met up with Bonneville. Sixty-four horses, 10 head of cattle, and 15 dogs had died on the return journey. However, all of Walker's men had survived the trip, and their only serious injury occurred when a California grizzly bear mangled one trapper.

* * *

Walker had a gift for geography. He brought back much information that contributed to the maps of the West. His route to California later became known as the California Trail and was used by thousands of emigrants.

Walker continued trapping in the Rocky Mountains. He worked for Bonneville, and later for the American Fur Company as a brigade leader.

After the 1837 summer rendezvous, Walker spent the winter in today's northern Arizona in territory that had never before been seen by white men. It is believed that Walker found gold in Arizona on this trip.

In 1840, Walker took an expedition south to Sevier Lake and to the Virgin River. This area is now covered by Lake Mead.

From 1840 to 1842, Walker bought horses, mules, and other trade goods in California, took them to Santa Fe and to the Rocky Mountains, and traded with the Spanish, the mountain men, and various Native American tribes.

Walker's wife was a member of the Snake tribe. They were together from 1836 to 1846. There is no record of her name.

In 1843 Walker guided the Chiles party to California. They were the first emigrants to use the California Trail and the first party to take wagons into California. They abandoned the wagons at the southern end of the Sierra Nevada, but Walker still got the party of fifty men, women, and children through Walker Pass ahead of a terrible blizzard.

Four months later, Walker was leaving California when he overtook John C. Frémont. Walker guided Frémont's party to Bent's Fort in present-day Colorado.

In 1845, Walker guided part of Frémont's third expedition to California. During a dispute between Frémont and the Mexicans, Frémont led his men to the top of Hawk's Peak. His men were prepared to fight, but when their flag fell down, Frémont took this as an "omen" and led his men out of the area.

Walker strongly disapproved. He called Frémont "the most complete coward I ever knew" and terminated his employment.

In 1846 Walker encountered the Donner party on the trail east of Fort Bridger. They told him they planned to take a shortcut to California called the

Joseph Walker's Snake (Shoshone) wife is shown here on horseback behind Walker.
The above painting was done by Alfred Jacob Miller.

Hastings Cutoff. When Walker advised against the route, they called him a "Missouri puke." They took the shortcut anyway, and about half the members of the party died as a result.

In 1850 Walker led an expedition to today's Zion National Park in southern Utah. They also explored in northern Arizona and spent several days with Zuni and Hopi peoples.

The next year, Walker led a party to find a direct route between Los Angeles and Albuquerque, approximately along the thirty-fifth parallel. They were the first white men to see parts of present-day central New Mexico and Arizona. In 1854, Walker took another expedition to explore the Mono Lake region of California.

Army Colonel William Hoffman hired Walker to guide his troops up the Colorado River in a campaign against the Mojaves in January 1859. Walker had traveled in the opposite direction, down the river, twenty years earlier. Nevertheless, each morning Walker made an accurate map of the territory they would cover that day. He marked good camping areas, as well as where they would find wood, water, and grass for the animals. Colonel Hoffman was astounded at Walker's remarkable memory.

Amazingly, Joseph Walker was still serving as a guide on various expeditions when he was in his seventies, as shown in this picture.

In 1861, a group of men hired Walker as their guide to explore for gold. Walker, who was then sixty-two years old, led the men through Death Valley, to the Colorado River, into the Rocky Mountains in Colorado, and south toward New Mexico. They prospected for gold in various places.

At the same time, twenty-four-year-old Daniel Conner was in Colorado and wanted to join Walker's party. He asked a friend which trail Walker had taken. The friend replied that Captain Walker does not follow trails, he makes them. Conner caught up to Walker's expedition in southern Colorado.

As they traveled to southern New Mexico, they were cautious to avoid the Apache. The country was rugged and barren and there was no water and no grazing. Walker assured the men they would find water at Cooke's Spring, which he had visited thirty years earlier.

As they traveled, the men began to doubt that Walker really remembered the spring's location after thirty years. But on the third day, Walker sent five men ahead to look for a square rock high on a mountainside. He said the spring was beneath that rock. Walker was right! The water was exactly where he said it would be.

In May 1863, this party found gold near today's Prescott, Arizona.

While Walker is now best remembered for the discovery of the Yosemite Valley, his intelligence, remarkable knowledge of geography, and his ability to lead his men and bring them back alive made him one of the most respected men in the West.

Walker died on October 27, 1876. He was almost seventy-eight years old.

CHAPTER 4
Mapping the Path for Manifest Destiny

◄►══◦◯══◦►◄►

The idea of Manifest Destiny has probably been around since the first caveman took over his neighbor's cave. Once he owned two caves, he expanded his ownership to three caves, then four, then . . . as many as possible. That fellow most likely believed in his heart that Providence intended for him to own more than just one cave.

That same idea continued through history. The fellow who owned many caves eventually became known as a master, a ruler, a dictator, a sheik, a governor, a king, a lord, or an emperor.

After the United States declared its independence in 1776, the founding fathers expected the new nation to grow. They believed Providence meant for the nation to take over more and more land.

However, Native American people were already living on that land. Even though their ancestors had lived there for at least ten thousand years, they would be forced to move over. The "civilized" farmers, ranchers, businesspeople, miners, and fence builders believed that *they* should control the land.

The idea of expanding westward received a name in 1845 when John L. O'Sullivan, editor of the New York newspaper *Democratic Review*, first used the term "Manifest Destiny." O'Sullivan wrote that it was America's "manifest destiny to overspread the continent allotted by Providence for the free development of our yearly multiplying millions."

Millions?

At first, there were only a few white people crossing the continent. The

EXPEDITIONS OF FRÉMONT (1842–1846)

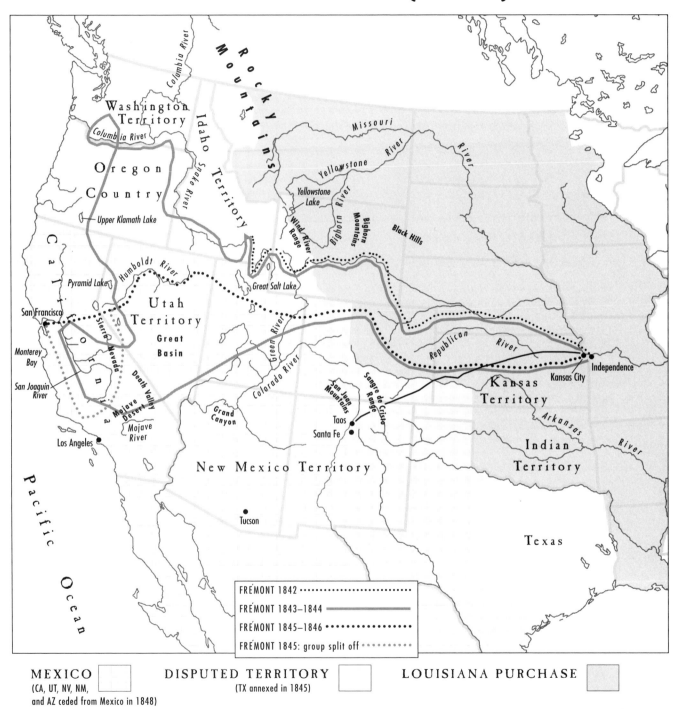

FRÉMONT 1842	··················
FRÉMONT 1843–1844	————————
FRÉMONT 1845–1846	●●●●●●●●●●●●
FRÉMONT 1845: group split off	∙∙∙∙∙∙∙∙∙∙∙∙

MEXICO
(CA, UT, NV, NM,
and AZ ceded from Mexico in 1848)

DISPUTED TERRITORY
(TX annexed in 1845)

LOUISIANA PURCHASE

Lewis and Clark Expedition had around forty men. Zebulon Pike and Stephen Long each had only around twenty men.

But after 1820, steamboats became more numerous on the Missouri and Mississippi rivers. Fur trappers scattered in every direction looking for beaver. In 1841, the first covered-wagon train moved settlers across the plains. By 1843, over a thousand emigrants had moved west. Then gold was discovered in California in 1848, and thousands of gold seekers rushed west.

This painting, entitled *American Progress* by John Gast, was created in 1873.
It has come to symbolize Manifest Destiny.

Buffalo, which were crucial to the survival of most of the plains tribes, were slaughtered by the thousands. White men carried devastating diseases to the native peoples, such as smallpox and cholera, which killed entire Native American villages. With the destruction of their cultures, languages, hunting ground, and means of survival, Native Americans paid an enormous price to fulfill John L. O'Sullivan's notion of Manifest Destiny.

JOHN C. FRÉMONT (1813-1890)

U.S. Army Officer, Surveyor, Mapmaker, Western Explorer, Author of Reports Encouraging Westward Expansion, Politician, Arizona Territory Governor, American Hero

John Charles Fremon (later Frémont) was almost eight months old when his unmarried parents spent the night of September 4, 1813, at City Hotel in Nashville, Tennessee.

That evening while baby John Charles slept, a disagreement broke out in the

While John Charles Frémont has been called the Pathfinder, most of the trails he traveled had already been discovered and used by others. However, Frémont made accurate maps and inspired many people to settle in the West.

hotel lobby between General Andrew Jackson and two brothers—Thomas Hart Benton and Jesse Benton. A fight developed, more people got involved, and guns were fired.

Jackson was seriously injured in the gunfire. Later it was discovered that one of the shots went through the wall and narrowly missed killing the sleeping baby John Charles Fremon.

No one could have known that night that baby John Charles would become Thomas Hart Benton's son-in-law twenty-eight years later, and that their lives would be forever joined by their belief in Manifest Destiny.

John Charles Fremon was born January 21, 1813. When he was five years old, his father died, leaving his mother to raise three children in poverty. After his father's death, a *t* was added to their last name. When John Charles was about twenty-five, he added an accent mark over the *e*.

John Charles grew up in Charleston, South Carolina, and he excelled in school. He attended Charleston College, but three months before graduation, Frémont skipped school and got expelled for "incorrigible negligence."

Frémont taught mathematics in private schools and aboard the USS *Natchez.* He also spent two years working as a surveyor.

Frémont was exceptionally ambitious and motivated to succeed. He found ways to meet rich and powerful men, including Joseph N. Nicollet, a French astronomer, mathematician, and explorer. Nicollet gave Frémont excellent training in surveying and mapmaking.

In 1838 and 1839, Frémont assisted Nicollet on mapping expeditions to the upper Mississippi and upper Missouri rivers, territory that Zebulon Pike and Stephen Long had traversed. Nicollet and Frémont took ninety thousand instrument readings and made three hundred twenty-six astronomical notes.

When they returned to Washington, they began work on their maps and reports. Senator Thomas Hart Benton, an important Congressman who supported American expansion into the West, visited their office and soon invited Frémont to his home.

When Frémont met Benton's sixteen-year-old daughter, he fell madly in love

Frémont met Jessie Benton when
she was sixteen years old.
They eloped in 1841, and she
remained his most loyal
supporter all her life.

with her. However, Jessie was eleven years younger than Frémont, and several other young men were courting her. Furthermore, her mother did not want Jessie to marry a poor army man.

To keep the two apart, Senator Benton arranged for Frémont to be sent on a six-month exploration of the Des Moines River. When Frémont returned, he and Jessie eloped. Senator Benton was furious, but after his anger cooled, he accepted Frémont into the family and became one of his greatest allies.

First Expedition: 1842

In the spring of 1842, Frémont received orders to command his first expedition: a survey of the Platte and Kansas rivers. No one knows for sure if he was told to go on to South Pass in the Rocky Mountains, but that's where he went.

Frémont assembled twenty-one voyageurs, a hunter, and a German cartographer and topographer named Charles Preuss. He also took along Henry Brant, a nineteen-year-old relative of the Benton family, and the Bentons' twelve-year-old son, Randolph, to prove that even a child could travel safely in the West.

Frémont took along instruments for mapping, a newly invented daguerreotype camera, and a newly invented inflatable India-rubber boat.

The party left Chouteau's trading post on June 10, 1842, near today's Kansas City, Missouri. Following the Oregon Trail along the Platte River, they traveled eleven miles the first day.

Frémont was strict about discipline, both for his men and himself. During midday stops and every evening, Frémont made careful astronomical observations. He kept a journal and recorded the plants and geological features of the region.

That same month, two Cheyenne men and a thirteen-year-old Cheyenne boy joined Frémont's camp. At first, Randolph Benton and the Cheyenne boy eyed each other suspiciously, but soon they became great friends.

Enormous herds of buffalo roamed the prairies. One herd had about eleven thousand animals. In places where there was no firewood because of a lack of trees, the party burned the large supply of *bois de vache*, which was dried buffalo dung.

The party met Jim Bridger on the trail. He warned that the Sioux, Blackfeet, and Cheyenne were on the warpath. Everyone knew the danger was serious when Kit Carson asked for someone who could read and write so that he could make out his will.

But Frémont was determined to proceed. However, he left Randolph Benton and Henry Brant at Fort Laramie, in present-day Wyoming, to their disappointment. He also told his men he wanted no cowards along, and he offered the option for anyone to drop out of the expedition. One man remained behind.

Frémont purchased a cone-shaped lodge, or tepee, while at Fort Laramie. Compared to a military tent, a tepee was more wind-resistant, warmer in winter, cooler in summer, and free from mosquitoes. On the first night away from Fort Laramie, Frémont's men struggled, clumsily trying to erect the lodge. Their Sioux guide's wife laughed at them, but she showed them how to set it up.

As they traveled, they met some Sioux warriors who had been on the warpath, but Frémont negotiated with them and there was no bloodshed. They

Thirty-three-year-old Kit Carson met John C. Frémont on a steamboat going up the Missouri River in 1842. Carson was already a trapper and a mountain man, as portrayed in the above picture. He guided most of Frémont's expeditions, and the two men became lifelong friends. Frémont's reports made Kit Carson a national hero.

also met some Arapaho and Cheyenne warriors who said they were headed home. Fortunately, they were not hostile.

The party crossed South Pass in present-day Wyoming and continued to the Wind River Range, where Frémont decided to climb the peak he thought was the highest in the Rocky Mountains. His men made a base camp, and Frémont left on August 12 with a party of fifteen men to climb the mountain.

The next day, the top of the mountain appeared near, so Frémont left the mules, provisions, and some of the men at a second camp. He took a few men to finish the hike on foot. Expecting to return before nightfall, they took no blankets, no coats, and no food. They carried only their scientific instruments, guns, and a flag.

As they climbed higher, several men, including Frémont, suffered violent headaches and began vomiting, signs of altitude sickness.

Each time the men thought they were near the top of the mountain, they realized there was a higher ridge. They constantly fell on the slippery, jagged rocks. But by evening, they had reached timberline and made camp. Cold and hungry, they spent a miserable night.

The next day, they continued their climb. Crossing ice- and snowfields, one man fell several hundred feet and landed on some rocks. Luckily, he was only bruised. Frémont and two others were so ill from the altitude and hunger that Frémont sent some of the men back to get blankets and food.

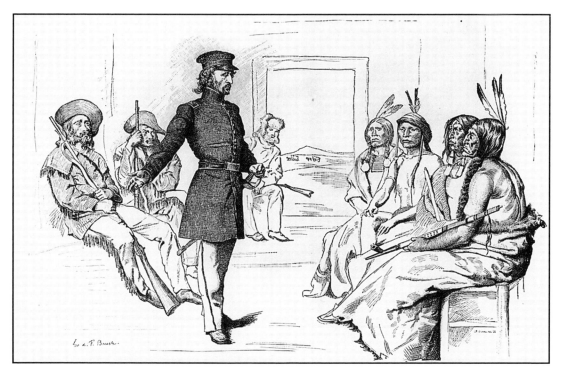

This picture is entitled *Frémont's Address to the Indians at Fort Laramie*.
Some of the chiefs to whom Frémont made this 1842 address included
Otter Hat, Breaker of Arrows, Black Night, and Bull's Tail.

The next morning, August 15, Frémont took five men with him to finish climbing. They took turns standing on the peak since it was only large enough for one man at a time. The men fired their pistols and cheered, and Frémont hoisted the flag he had brought just for that purpose.

The peak they climbed is not the highest peak in the Rocky Mountains. Now called Woodrow Wilson Peak, it's not even the highest mountain in the Wind River Range. There's a higher peak about five miles away!

On the trip home, Frémont divided the party. While some of the men went overland, Frémont and six others inflated the rubber boat and floated down the North Platte River. They ran the first set of rapids with no problems. The next rapids were more dangerous, but they shot through them as well. Again and again,

On the morning of August 15, 1842, Frémont and five men climbed to the top of what Frémont thought was the highest peak in the Rocky Mountains.

the boat plunged over waterfalls. The ride was exciting, and the men shouted and sang Canadian boat songs as they rode one set of rapids after another.

Suddenly, the boat hit a rock and upset, dumping men and gear into the water. Although three of the men could not swim, no one lost his life. But journals, notebooks, blankets, clothing, food, plant and mineral specimens, notes, guns, ammunition, the raft, the daguerreotype camera, and the scientific instruments were swept downstream. They lost all of their scientific records. Amazingly, some of Frémont's books and Preuss's journal were later pulled from the river.

The party returned to Fort Laramie on August 31, and arrived in St. Louis October 17.

Frémont immediately began working on his report. Writing gave him headaches and nosebleeds, so Jessie offered to help. Frémont would pace back and forth as he dictated, and Jessie wrote the notes. He included information about the various Native American tribes, the trails, weather, and finding wood, campsites, water, and game.

Frémont disagreed with Zebulon Pike and Stephen Long's reports about "the Great American Desert." His report indicated that the states of Kansas and Nebraska were not desert wastelands, but fertile lands on which crops or live-stock could be raised.

With Frémont's enthusiasm and his gift for making the West seem romantic, plus Jessie's writing ability, the report read like a novel. The U.S. Senate ordered one thousand extra copies. Private publishers issued copies for the public.

Second Expedition: 1843–1844

Frémont's assignment for his second expedition was to extend his 1842 survey to the Pacific Ocean.

In May 1843, Frémont headed west with a party of thirty-nine men, including Kit Carson; Charles Preuss, the topographer; Jacob Dodson, an eighteen-year-old free black man; and two Delaware Native Americans.

The surveying equipment included a refracting telescope, a reflecting circle, two sextants, two pocket chronometers, six thermometers, small compasses, and two barometers. Frémont also took along another daguerreotype camera, another rubber boat, and a brass mountain howitzer, a kind of cannon.

The party reached the Great Salt Lake on September 6, and Frémont took five men to explore it. Two cylinders on their inflatable boat leaked, so one man constantly pumped bellows to keep air in them.

When they returned to the main camp, Frémont boiled five gallons of lake water over the campfire. Once the water boiled away, fourteen pints of salt remained. They carried the salt along to season their food.

As they traveled toward the Northwest, the Native Americans they met were much different from those of the plains and Rocky Mountains. One Snake tribe provided Frémont's men with plenty of salmon, lively talk, and loud laughter. Another group dressed in an unusual manner, as they had recently traded their salmon for pieces of emigrants' clothing. One man wore a shirt; another, an overcoat; another, pantaloons.

Frémont reached Fort Vancouver, in present-day Washington State, in November. Dr. John McLoughlin was in charge of the fort, and he welcomed Frémont and sold him flour, peas, tallow, horses, mules, and cattle.

Frémont collected information on the topography, geology, botany, zoology, soil, and water. He mapped and determined the heights of Mount Hood, Mount Rainier, and Mount St. Helens. He saw two volcanoes, Mount St. Helens and Mount Baker, erupt.

A nineteen-year-old Chinook joined Frémont's expedition. He could speak a few words of English and was eager to see how the whites lived.

Fort Vancouver was as far as Frémont had been assigned to explore. But he wasn't finished. With 25 men, 2 Wasco guides, some cattle, and 104 mules and horses, Frémont left the Columbia River valley on November 25, 1843, and went south to Klamath Lake.

On December 16, the temperature was around zero degrees as they traveled through a storm and three feet of snow. About noon, they came out of a forest at the edge of a cliff. Even though a snowstorm raged around them, a thousand feet below they could see a green prairie, a beautiful lake, and sunshine. Frémont named the lake Summer Lake, and that name is still used.

They traveled along the rim several miles before finding a place where they could descend to the valley. One mule lost its footing and rolled over and over for about three hundred feet. Amazingly, the animal stood up and made its way down the steep, rocky wall. It was fine except for some scrapes and bruises and a lost pack.

It was dark by the time all the men, animals, and equipment were together on the valley floor.

A week later, on Christmas morning of 1843, they camped beside another lake, which Frémont named Christmas Lake. It is either present-day Hart Lake or Crump Lake. By this time, they were in the desert. Frémont described it as a "remote, desolate land." Having to spend Christmas in such isolated, barren, and forbidding land, the men's spirits were low, so Frémont poured everyone a drink of brandy to toast the day. Louis Zindel fired the cannon and the rest of the men fired their pistols. They had coffee *with* sugar, then continued their journey.

They were in Paiute country, but for a long time they didn't actually see any Native Americans. However, the Paiute could see them! The warriors moved stealthily and stole two horses during the night. The night watchmen did not hear or see a thing.

A week later, in present-day Nevada, the party awoke to a thick fog. Several men went to get the horses and wandered around for hours, unable to find their way back to camp. The fog lasted four days.

They had eaten the last of the cattle that they had brought from Fort Vancouver. Only eighty-nine pack animals were still alive. Some had been stolen by Native Americans, but the others had died. The surviving horses and mules were suffering from lameness and horribly cut feet caused by the rocky terrain.

Frémont knew the animals could not continue across the desert to the Rocky Mountains. So on January 18, 1844, he announced that the group would go to California. His men cheered. The next day, they turned west to cross the Sierra Nevada and immediately ran into heavy snow and rugged terrain.

At the end of January, they encountered a tribe of Washo that gave Frémont's

On January 10, 1844, Frémont discovered a lake, which he named Pyramid Lake
because of the strangely shaped rock protruding from the water.
Charles Preuss drew the scene in the picture above. A detail from the painting is
shown here. The cannon Frémont hauled across the country is shown beside Frémont's
cone-shaped lodge.

party pine nuts to eat. The Washo advised against crossing the mountains in the
snow. When Frémont insisted, one young man agreed to serve as a guide, but he
deserted after two days.

On January 29, they finally abandoned the howitzer that two mules had
pulled across the continent. The men were sad to part with it, considering it an
old friend!

They met more Washo the next day and another young man agreed to guide
them. To entice him to stay, Frémont gave him leggings, moccasins, a large green
blanket, and blue and scarlet cloth.

By the first of February, they were down to sixty-seven horses and mules,
and in serious trouble. They were out of meat, so Frémont gave the cook permission to prepare a pet dog for dinner.

The next day, the men began digging through snow to break a trail. To avoid the snow-filled valleys, they cleared roads for the animals on the sides of the steep mountains. In one spot, the terrified animals left the trail and plunged into snowdrifts up to their ears.

Some slopes were so steep that the animals slipped on the ice and slid hundreds of yards down the mountain until they bumped into a tree or rock. Then the men had to go down the side of the mountain and help the animals back up to the trail.

This illustration, entitled *Pass in the Sierra Nevada*, was made by
Charles Preuss, the topographer on Frémont's expedition. A detail of it is shown here.
Snow fell constantly while the party crossed the Sierra Nevada.
The men were exhausted, frostbitten, and hungry.

On the night of February 4, two more Washo men joined their camp. Some of Frémont's men had learned a few words of their language. One old man warned them they were bound for a cold and miserable death if they continued over the mountains. The next morning all the Washos were gone—even the guide had deserted.

On February 5, Frémont ordered some of his men to begin building sledges on which to move their gear. They also made snowshoes similar to those the Washo wore.

A few men used black silk handkerchiefs to protect their eyes from the glare of the snow, but the others suffered from the pain of being snowblind.

By February 17, the party was down to fifty-seven animals. To keep from starving, they killed a mule almost every day.

They reached the summit of the pass on February 20. As they started down the next day, the weather got a little warmer, but that only made conditions worse. As the snow's crust melted, the men and the animals sank into deep snowdrifts, slipped on wet rocks, or slid on melting ice.

Three days later, the snow was so slippery that the men had to crawl on hands and knees to make a path for the animals. Many horses and mules fell over the side of the mountain. Several were carrying packs, and they lost all the plant specimens that had been collected along two thousand miles of the trail.

The hardships were taking a toll on the men's minds. On February 27, Charles Town was, as Frémont described him, "suffering from lightheadedness" and wandered into the woods. Jacob Dodson found him and brought him back to camp. Two days later, Town dived into the icy river and began swimming as though it were summer. Another man jumped in and pulled him out.

The next day, Baptiste Derosier went to look for a lost horse and was gone for over thirty hours. He lost track of time and didn't know where he was. When he rejoined the party, Frémont wrote that he was "deranged."

On March 8, the expedition finally arrived at John Sutter's fort, the place where gold would be discovered in 1848 and start the California gold rush. Only thirty-three animals had survived crossing the Sierra Nevada.

After the men recovered from their ordeal, they re-outfitted with one hundred thirty horses and mules and thirty head of cattle. The party set out again on March 24 and went south. They followed the old Spanish Trail to cross the desert.

A month later, a Mexican man and a boy came into Frémont's camp. Andreas Fuentes and eleven-year-old Pablo Hernandez said a band of Paiutes had stolen their thirty horses and killed four other people, including Pablo's parents.

Kit Carson and Alexis Godey followed the trail to the Paiutes' encampment. They killed two men and brought the two scalps back to camp, as well as most of the stolen horses.

Frémont took charge of caring for Pablo. Three days later, Pablo sobbed for his dead mother and father when the party reached the springs where they had died. The family's small dog had stayed with the bodies, and it was very happy to see Pablo again.

As they crossed the Mojave desert, it was often fifty to sixty miles between water springs. The skeletons of horses from earlier expeditions lay beside the trail. On May 4 the party traveled into the night to avoid the heat. About midnight, the mules began running. They had caught the scent of water!

By the time they reached the springs at present-day Las Vegas, Nevada, their surviving horses and mules were suffering from hunger, from thirst, and from the volcanic rock gouging their hooves. Frémont ordered a day's rest.

The next morning, a band of Southern Paiutes surrounded their camp and threatened to attack. Using diplomacy, Frémont avoided a battle.

On May 9, near today's Littlefield, Arizona, Baptiste Tabeau backtracked to search for a lost mule. He was alone and the Paiutes killed him. Tabeau's murder brought grief and anger to the entire party.

Three days later, Joseph Walker overtook Frémont near present-day New-castle, Utah. Thomas Fitzpatrick and Kit Carson, who were Frémont's guides, were glad to see their old friend. Since Walker had traveled through the Great Basin more than anyone, Frémont hired him as chief guide.

As they crossed present-day Utah, Frémont made a major error. He recorded that Utah Lake was an arm of Great Salt Lake.

From Utah, they went into northern Colorado, south through Colorado, east to Bent's Fort, and returned to St. Louis on August 6, 1844, after a fourteen-month journey.

Newspapers called Frémont a national hero. He brought back scientific specimens and information about geologic formations. His map was the first truly scientific map of the West. With Jessie's assistance, Frémont wrote a six-hundred-page report. It wasn't written only for scientists and Congress: It was a guidebook for common people crossing the continent. It included information on trails, distances, finding wood and water, hiring guides, and services at various forts.

Frémont described the land and included hardships such as mosquitoes, bears, rattlesnakes, extreme weather, storms, difficult terrain, and miles with no water, no grazing for the animals, and no game. He suggested avoiding problems with the various tribes by providing gifts in exchange for the privilege of crossing their lands.

The U.S. Senate published ten thousand copies of Frémont's report. A commercial publisher also brought out an edition for the public. Six printings were made. It was truly a best seller.

Frémont was promoted from first lieutenant to captain.

Third Expedition: 1845–1846

Frémont's written orders for his third expedition were to survey the Arkansas and Red rivers. This seems strange because the region had already been explored. The orders did not mention California, yet Frémont headed there. Later, he claimed he had received verbal orders to go to California.

The expedition left Independence, Missouri, on June 20, 1845, with sixty men and two hundred horses and mules. In August, they stopped at Bent's Fort, where Frémont once again hired Joseph Walker as a guide.

The party traveled around Great Salt Lake to the river Frémont officially named the Humboldt. There the expedition divided and took different routes. The two groups rejoined in California in the middle of February 1846.

Frémont requested permission from the Mexican authorities to enter California. He said he was on a surveying assignment and that his mission was in the

After Frémont's second expedition, he was a national hero. Everywhere he went,
men asked to be selected to accompany him on the third journey. Once the third expedition
began, the new recruits had to learn the art of packing and handling mules,
as shown in the illustration above.

interest of science and trade. The officials did not believe him, but they granted
him permission to re-outfit.

Soon there was a dispute over a stolen horse. Then some of Frémont's men got
drunk and insulted the governor's family. During the first week of March, General
Jose Castro ordered Frémont to leave California. In defiance, Frémont led his
party to the top of Hawk's Peak in the Gavilan Mountains. They raised the American flag, but after three days the flagpole and flag fell down. Frémont interpreted
this as a bad omen and retreated to the San Joaquin and Sacramento valleys.

In the middle of April, some Americans who had moved to California asked
Frémont for protection from the local Native Americans. While Frémont did
not get involved, Kit Carson led an attack. In three hours, 175 Wintun and Yana
people were murdered.

The inset in this image portrays Frémont's encampment in the Sacramento Valley. Frémont is shown in the portrait wearing his military uniform.

The next week, Frémont moved his party north to Klamath Lake in Oregon. On the night of May 9, Frémont failed to assign anyone guard duty, and a band of Native Americans snuck into the camp. Frémont's party awoke and drove off the warriors, killing their chief. But the Native Americans had killed three of Frémont's men.

Angry, Frémont and Carson led an attack on the largest nearby village. They killed over two dozen Klamath people and set the village on fire. It is believed the original attack party was a band of Modocs and that these Klamath people had nothing to do with killing Frémont's men.

When the expedition returned to California, they discovered General Castro had ordered all non-Mexican citizens out of California. Rumors circulated that Castro had told the Maidus to kill any remaining Americans. Frémont became

On the night of May 9, 1846, three of Frémont's men were killed when a band of warriors snuck into the camp. Among those killed was Basil Lajenesse, who had been on all of Frémont's expeditions. On May 12, Frémont ordered an attack on the largest Klamath village, as shown in the above illustration, a detail of which is shown here. His men killed over two dozen Klamath people and set the village on fire, without finding out if these people had actually attacked their camp.

suspicious and began raiding the Maidu villages, killing men, women, and children in surprise attacks.

At the same time, the American settlers considered it their right to settle in California. Calling themselves Osos, which is Spanish for bears, they took control of the village of Sonoma. They made a flag with a bear on it. Their uprising was called the Bear Flag Revolt.

In the last week of June, Frémont moved his men to Sonoma. He later defended his actions, claiming that, as an officer in the army, he was protecting the Osos, who were American citizens.

Ten days later, Frémont became leader of the volunteer army that called itself the California Battalion of Volunteers. He led the troops to Monterey. At the same time, Commodore Robert F. Stockton took command of the naval forces in the port at Monterey. Stockton appointed Frémont to the rank of major. Frémont marched south. Without any battles or bloodshed, he captured Los Angeles. That fall Commodore Stockton promoted Frémont to lieutenant colonel.

In January 1847, Frémont negotiated a treaty at the Mission San Fernando to bring a peaceful ending to the war. Commodore Stockton then named Frémont governor of California.

Meanwhile, Brigadier General Stephen Kearny arrived in California with his troops. Kearny reprimanded Stockton and a feud erupted over who was in command. The two issued conflicting orders to Frémont. Frémont decided to obey Stockton's orders.

But Frémont was in the army, not the navy, making Kearny his commanding officer. Since Frémont disobeyed his commanding officer's orders, Brigadier General Kearny arrested him. Kearny's party, with Frémont under arrest, left California in June. Even though Frémont returned to St. Louis in disgrace, crowds gathered beside the river and cheered him.

Frémont was court-martialed and charged with disobeying orders, mutiny, and conduct to the prejudice of good order and military discipline. He was found guilty on all three counts.

In a strange twist, President James Knox Polk remitted the sentence and ordered Frémont restored to active duty. But Frémont refused the pardon, since that would have been an acknowledgment of guilt. He insisted he was innocent. Bitter, he resigned from the army.

Even though Frémont had been court-martialed, he wrote his report, which became important in the development of the West.

Fourth Expedition: 1848–1849

Frémont was eager to put the court-martial behind him and looked for work outside the military. At the same time, some wealthy St. Louis businessmen wanted to put a railroad through from St. Louis to California. Frémont was selected to find a route following the thirty-eighth parallel.

There were concerns about the snowy mountains and the Ute tribes, but Frémont was convinced there would be no difficulties. He planned the expedition for the winter to prove it was safe. He claimed the entire journey to California would take only thirty-five days.

The men who financed the expedition would not pay wages, but they furnished supplies and 120 horses and mules. Frémont's party of 35 volunteers left St. Louis on October 4, 1848, and arrived at Bent's Fort on November 15. A foot of snow was on the ground and the temperature was twelve degrees.

Frémont tried to hire a guide, but no one wanted the job. The Native Americans and mountain men at the fort predicted a hard winter, and warned against going into the mountains. But Frémont would not be discouraged. He moved his party up to present-day Pueblo, Colorado. There a sixty-two-year-old trapper named Old Bill Williams agreed to guide them.

The party left Hardscrabble, the last settlement in Colorado, on November 25. They went through the Wet Mountains and the Sangre de Cristo Mountains. Temperatures dropped and heavy snow fell. The men's beards, eyelashes, and hair were white with frost. Their breath formed ice on their faces and they could hardly speak.

On December 3, they trudged through five inches of new snow across Robidoux Pass. Coming out of the Sangre de Cristos, they passed the area now known as Great Sand Dunes.

That night, the wind whipped the snow and the temperature dropped to seventeen degrees below zero. While the men slept, the mules returned to the mountains to find shelter and shrubbery to eat. In the middle of the night, the men had to find their way in the dark to retrieve the wayward mules. The next day, they waded in waist-deep freezing water to force their mules across a creek.

Old Bill Williams recommended that the party go south into New Mexico and avoid the mountains. But Frémont was determined to follow the thirty-eighth parallel and did not heed his guide's advice.

The Cochetopa Pass was a known route across the Continental Divide, and was probably the pass Frémont intended to use. However, the party made a wrong turn toward a more difficult route called Wagon Wheel Gap. This was probably the fault of Old Bill Williams.

During the second week of December, they made it into the San Juan Mountains. The snow was three to four feet deep as they made their way along the side walls of one narrow canyon. One day it took them an hour and a half to climb a three-hundred-foot hill through snow that was fifteen feet deep.

That night, one of Dr. Benjamin Kern's socks had frozen to his foot and had to be thawed before he could pull it off. On December 14, eight mules froze and starved to death. Seven more perished the next day.

On December 16, Dr. Kern's eyelids froze closed, and for a while he could only see red. The next day his mule stopped, refusing to take another step. Dr. Kern pushed the animal with his knee and it fell over dead.

For six days, the party stayed by a creek and named the place Camp Desolation. Dead mules were scattered around the camp.

At the high altitude, every step was an effort, and many of the men suffered severe nosebleeds. Altitude sickness affected Frémont's thinking. Even Old Bill Williams was so cold he didn't make sense.

By December 20, over half the mules had died. The snow was thirty feet deep, and in some canyons, it was one hundred feet deep. Temperatures fell to twenty degrees below zero. The wind's howl was so loud the men could not hear above the roar. They could not see into the driving snow.

For a short time, the storm broke. Ahead of them was nothing but mountain ranges and valleys buried in snow. Frémont realized going farther was impos-

During Frémont's fourth expedition, the mules were so weak they fell over on the trail. Often the men had to put an animal down, as illustrated in this picture by Frederic Remington, which accompanied a magazine article by Thomas Breckenridge.

sible. Although turning around was equally difficult, on December 22, Frémont ordered a retreat.

They made a trail back over the divide and camped beside a creek. It took three days to move all the baggage and equipment. This is where they spent Christmas.

The men built huge fires, but the flames melted the snow beneath them, creating pits so deep, the men huddling next to one fire could not see over the snow to men huddling around another.

On December 26, Frémont sent his four "stoutest men" to go for help: Henry King as the leader, William Creutzfeldt, Tom Breckenridge, and Old Bill Williams. They were to follow the Rio Grande into New Mexico, a journey of 160 miles. Frémont expected them to return in sixteen days.

Meanwhile, the other men began moving the gear toward the Rio Grande.

The names of their camps reflected their spirits—Camp Hope, Camp Disappointment, and Camp Desolation. There was no game, so the men boiled their rawhide ropes and leather bags to make soup. They were starving, and each day they became weaker.

On January 9 Raphael Proue lay down in the snow to rest and froze to death. Frémont became angry. He said Proue had betrayed him by giving up. The men were too weak to bury his body. Besides, the ground was thirty feet beneath the snow's surface.

In 1896, Thomas Breckenridge related the story of Frémont's fourth expedition. He included a bit of humor by describing their Christmas dinner menu. This was probably the only humor to come from the tragic expedition of 1848-1849.

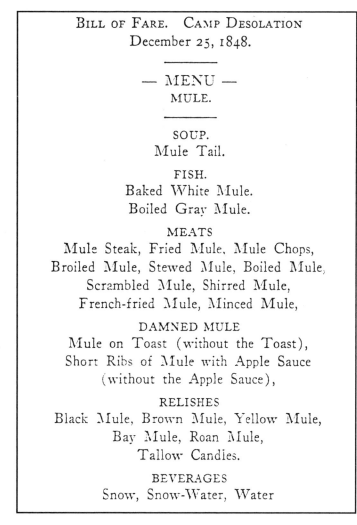

BILL OF FARE. CAMP DESOLATION
December 25, 1848.

— MENU —
MULE.

SOUP.
Mule Tail.

FISH.
Baked White Mule.
Boiled Gray Mule.

MEATS
Mule Steak, Fried Mule, Mule Chops,
Broiled Mule, Stewed Mule, Boiled Mule,
Scrambled Mule, Shirred Mule,
French-fried Mule, Minced Mule,

DAMNED MULE
Mule on Toast (without the Toast),
Short Ribs of Mule with Apple Sauce
(without the Apple Sauce),

RELISHES
Black Mule, Brown Mule, Yellow Mule,
Bay Mule, Roan Mule,
Tallow Candles.

BEVERAGES
Snow, Snow-Water, Water

Sixteen days after King's rescue party left to find help, Frémont decided they had either gotten lost or been killed. So on January 11, Frémont took four men with him to get help. He put Lorenzo Vincenthaler in charge of moving the remainder of the party toward New Mexico.

As it turned out, the group sent ahead on December 26 endured unbelievable hardships. On the third day, they ate the last of their food and their candles. Over the next two weeks, they ate a dead otter, killed one hawk, and roasted their belts, knife scabbards, boots, and moccasins. They wrapped their frostbitten feet in blankets. At night, they put their feet together and covered their heads with their blankets. Each day they grew weaker and suffered the pain of snowblindness.

On January 12, King sat down to rest, saying he would catch up later. The other three found a clump of trees and made a fire, then Creutzfeldt returned to help King to camp. But King was already dead. Creutzfeldt went a little crazy. Some reports indicate the starving men ate part of King's body.

On January 16, Frémont caught up with the three men. He said they were the most miserable objects he had ever seen. Luckily, Frémont had met some Utes who had four horses and agreed to help his men.

They moved south to a tiny village known today as Questa, New Mexico, and then they moved on to Taos. Frémont was frostbitten and ill, so he went to Kit Carson's home nearby. He did not return to help his men. Alexis Godey left Taos almost immediately with some Mexicans and Native Americans who were willing to help get supplies and mules to the stranded party.

Meanwhile, the men Frémont had left behind on January 11 were in terrible condition, with only rawhide ropes and candles to eat. Vincenthaler, the leader, had ordered the men to move the expedition's baggage. The group began to separate.

Manual, a California Native American who had joined Frémont's second expedition, had feet so severly frostbitten that the flesh had rotted off. He begged Vincenthaler to shoot him, but Vincenthaler refused. Juan and Gregorio, two other California men, brought Manual some firewood before leaving him alone.

In 1896, *Cosmopolitan Magazine* published Thomas Breckenridge's story of Frémont's fourth expedition. Frederic Remington made the above illustration to accompany the article. The caption reads, "We awoke early, stirred the fire."

On January 17, Henry Wise lay down beside the trail and died. The next day, Carver began raving, then wandered away from camp. No one ever saw him again.

When a deer was shot, Vincenthaler gave the stronger men a larger share than he gave the weaker.

Vincent Tabeau and Antoine Morin moved down the river, disappeared, and were never seen again.

On January 21, Vincenthaler announced he would no longer be in command. He and nine other men moved ahead. Over a period of five days, the men who had been left behind survived on two grouse, part of a rotten wolf carcass, some water beetles, rosebuds, their moccasin soles, and a skin sack.

Elijah Andrews died on January 24, and the next day Henry Rohrer thrashed for a while, then died, too. There were rumors that these two bodies were cannibalized. Benjamin Beadle and George Hubbard died two days later.

On January 24, Alexis Godey's rescue party reached the first survivors with the lifesaving provisions. Godey rescued the surviving men at various points along the trail. As he rode up to one haggard group, the men thought he was Frémont and they saluted, then broke down and wept. All the survivors reached Taos by February 11. Ten of the original thirty-three men had died. This was among the worst tragedies in the history of western exploration.

As soon as the survivors returned to Taos, Frémont organized a new outfit to go to California. Twenty-five men volunteered. Many were the survivors who had just been rescued from the mountains which is proof of Frémont's charisma and strong leadership qualities. This expedition left on February 13 and went through southern Arizona and into California.

Benjamin Kern and Old Bill Williams remained behind and tried to recover the equipment left in the mountains. They were killed by Ute warriors. A legend says that when the Utes realized whom they had killed, they gave Old Bill Williams a chief's funeral.

Frémont's fourth expedition put him ten thousand dollars in debt.

When Frémont reached Sutter's Fort, the 1849 gold rush had begun. Frémont owned land at the foot of the Sierra Nevada, and gold was discovered on it. At one point, Frémont was worth ten million dollars. He later lost his money through bad business investments.

In 1850, the California Legislature elected Frémont to be one of the state's first U.S. senators.

Fifth Expedition: 1853–1854

By 1853, there was still no railroad across the continent. Senator Benton arranged private financing for Frémont to lead another expedition to California.

The route Frémont proposed through Colorado's San Juan Mountains was not new. But Frémont planned to go in the middle of winter again to prove that a railway could operate year-round on his route.

With 22 men, Frémont left St. Louis in September, 1853. On the first of November on the Kansas River, a prairie fire threatened their camp. The only escape was to ride through the blazing grass. Everyone got through the flames safely.

Frémont always assigned guards. Early in the expedition, he discovered that one of the guards had left his post and returned to get warm by the campfire. At daybreak, they realized some Cheyenne had stolen five pack animals while the man was away from his watch. Frémont punished the guard by making him walk the next day.

They reached Bent's Fort at the end of November, entered the Wet Mountains on December 3, went through the Sangre de Cristo Mountains, crossed the San Luis Valley, and reached Cochetopa Pass on December 14. This was a milder winter than the 1848–1849 winter had been.

In Grand Valley, one of the pack mules lost its footing and fell down the side of the mountain. Like a chain, one animal after another fell over the mountainside. One horse and one mule were killed, but amazingly, many of the animals were uninjured.

Hunger was the party's worst problem. As their horses and mules died of starvation, the men ate every part of the animals. They made soup of the entrails, and burned the hair off the hide and roasted it till it was crisp.

After hearing rumors of cannibalism on his fourth expedition, Frémont made the men take an oath that if someone died, no one would eat him. Anyone who broke that promise would be shot. Everyone agreed.

By February 5, 1854, the party had reached the southern Utah mountains. The snow was so deep they had to assist the few animals that were still alive. Everyone was discouraged, but Frémont promised there was a town three days ahead.

On February 7, Oliver Fuller died. But the next day, the party came out of the mountains and into Parowan, Utah. The four hundred Mormons living there

In this image, Frémont and Solomon Carvalho take astronomical observations on Frémont's fifth and final expedition. Even in the terrible cold, Frémont sometimes stood in snow up to his waist to take the readings.

opened their homes to the men and fed them. Frémont's party stayed for two weeks.

Two men dropped out of the expedition. The others headed west and arrived in San Francisco on April 16. This was Frémont's last expedition. When he returned to New York, he mapped a route for a railroad line, but the route was never used.

* * *

In 1856, Frémont was the new Republican Party's first candidate for president of the United States, but he lost to James Buchanan.

Frémont served for a short time as a general in the Union army during the Civil War, and was governor of the Arizona Territory from 1878 to 1881.

Frémont was not a good businessman. He died in New York on July 13, 1890, impoverished and unknown. Jessie Benton Frémont died in 1902. Three of their children survived to adulthood.

The newly formed Republican Party used Frémont's experience as an explorer and soldier in his campaign for president of the United States. Frémont lost to James Buchanan.

CHAPTER 5
Surveying the Vast West

❖❖❖

When the United States bought the western land called the Louisiana Purchase, no one knew for certain exactly what the deal included. Through the years, many explorers collected information about the region known as the West, but by the time the Civil War began, there were still many unknowns.

Beginning in 1860, what has become known as the great surveys began. Josiah Dwight Whitney led the California survey from 1860 to 1870.

In 1867 Clarence King, who had been a member of Whitney's team, conducted the U.S. survey of the fortieth parallel. King mapped the proposed route for the transcontinental railroad from the Sierra Nevada through the Rocky Mountains.

Army Lieutenant George Montague Wheeler led the United States Geographical Surveys West of the One Hundredth Meridian. From 1867 to 1879, Wheeler explored and mapped more than a quarter of the United States west of the one-hundredth meridian, including the deserts of the Great Basin, Death Valley, and the western part of the Grand Canyon.

After the Civil War, Ferdinand V. Hayden began a survey of Nebraska. In 1869, he was made head of the United States Geological Survey of the Territories, mapping parts of what is now Colorado, Wyoming, Montana, and Idaho.

All of these surveys not only mapped the regions, but also gathered information about the geology and mineral resources of the West.

There was another man collecting this information as well, and at first he was doing his work without government funding. He would become one of the most

EXPEDITIONS OF POWELL (1869–1872)

POWELL 1869	··········
HAWKINS & HALL 1869	——————
POWELL 1871–1872	··········

Oregon

Idaho Territory

Wyoming Territory

R o c k y   M o u n t a i n s

Snake River

Great Salt Lake

● Salt Lake City

Utah Territory

Nevada

Great Basin

California

Flaming Gorge

Green River

Desolation Canyon

Disaster Falls

Colorado

Dirty Devil River

Henry Mountains

Escalante River

Glen Canyon

Marble Canyon

River

Virgin

Mojave Desert

Colorado River

River

Grand Canyon

Serpentine Falls

The Crossing of the Fathers

Little Colorado River

Sangre de Cristo Range

Arizona Territory

New Mexico Territory

Pacific Ocean

Gulf of California

LOUISIANA PURCHASE

knowledgeable and influential men of the Great American West: John Wesley Powell.

JOHN WESLEY POWELL (1834-1902)

U.S. Army Officer, Professor, Surveyor, Geologist, Explorer, First White Man to Descend the Colorado River Through the Grand Canyon, Ethnologist, Anthropologist, Director of Two U.S. Government Bureaus

Not many people live long enough to read their own obituary. But John Wesley Powell did. His 1869 expedition down the Colorado River was so dangerous that when a man named John A. Risdon said that the whole party had drowned, a lot of people believed him. Newspapers interviewed Risdon, published his story, and ran Powell's obituary.

But John A. Risdon was a fraud, and John Wesley Powell was later able to read the greatly exaggerated reports of his own death.

* * *

John Wesley Powell helped establish the U.S. Geological Survey and was its director from 1881 to 1894. He was also the first director of the U.S. Bureau of Ethnology.

John Wesley Powell was born on March 24, 1834, in Mount Morris, New York, the oldest of eight children. The family moved to Ohio when Wes, as his family called him, was four. Wes's father was an abolitionist, and other families disagreed with his views. When Wes was eight, boys at school threw stones at him. His mother was afraid he would be injured, so she took him out of school.

George Crookham, a neighbor and a self-taught scientist, offered to tutor Wes. Crookham had a library of works of science and literature, and he had made collections of Native American relics and natural history specimens. He introduced Wes to geology and archaeology, and took him along on field trips to caves, quarries, mines, and prehistoric mounds.

In 1846, the Powells moved to Wisconsin. Since Wes's father was a circuit-riding preacher and was away much of the time, twelve-year-old Wes managed the farm. There were no schools in the area, so Wes borrowed science books and read constantly. He began his own collections of flowers, insects, and Native American relics.

In May 1847, Wes and his mother visited a tribe of Winnebagos camped near the Powell farm. For the rest of his life, Powell was fascinated by Native Americans.

When Wes was eighteen years old, he began teaching in a one-room school in Wisconsin. Over the next seven years, he alternated between teaching school and attending various colleges, but he never graduated from any of them.

When Powell was in his early twenties, he traveled alone by boat on the Mississippi, Ohio, Illinois, and Des Moines rivers, collecting plants, shells, and minerals. In 1861, he married his cousin Emma.

The Civil War broke out that same year, and Powell enlisted in the Twentieth Illinois Volunteer Infantry. He was rapidly promoted to the rank of captain in the Union army, and fought at the Battle of Shiloh. On April 6, 1862, he raised his right arm to give a signal and was hit by a minié ball. It shattered his arm, and the doctors later amputated it below the elbow.

Although he now had only one arm, Powell continued as a Union officer and fought at the siege of Vicksburg, Mississippi. He was promoted to the rank of major, and, for the rest of his life he was addressed as Major Powell.

Although Powell was an army officer, he never stopped being a scientist.

When the trenches were dug around Vicksburg, he collected fossils as they were unearthed. And while in Louisiana, he gathered a collection of mollusks.

After the war, Powell became a university professor, lecturer, museum curator, and secretary of the Illinois Natural History Society.

In the summers of 1867 and 1868, Powell took groups of students, biologists, and amateur naturalists, including his wife, on field trips to the Rocky Mountains. In 1867, the group climbed Pikes Peak. In 1868, Powell and six other men were the first white men to climb Longs Peak.

Powell was intrigued by the Colorado and Green rivers, which were in one of the last unmapped regions of the West. Mountain men claimed the canyons were impassable. They told stories of men who had died going down the Colorado River in boats. Some native peoples feared the river and believed the gods had made it impassable so that man would not go down it. They also believed anyone that entered the canyon would be punished.

In 1856, John Wesley Powell traveled to Detroit to meet his uncle Joseph. During the visit, he fell in love with his cousin Emma. Their families opposed a marriage because they were first cousins, but they married anyway in November 1861.

John Wesley Powell fought in the Civil War, as illustrated above. At the Battle of Shiloh, a minié ball shattered his right arm, and the doctors amputated it below the elbow. He suffered pain from that accident for the rest of his life.

As Powell traveled, he met five men who wanted to run the river with him. Beyond descending it, Powell planned to map the river and gather geological and natural history data.

First Expedition: 1869

Powell returned to the East in the fall of 1868 to raise money and prepare for the journey. He designed four specially reinforced boats with watertight compartments, and had them built in Chicago. He convinced the Union Pacific Railroad to transport the boats to Green River, Wyoming, without charge.

The pilot boat was sixteen feet long, weighed less than the other boats, and could be maneuvered more easily. The other three boats were each twenty-one feet long, weighed almost a thousand pounds, and could hold a ton of cargo.

Powell took enough supplies for a ten-month expedition: food (bacon, beans, flour, sugar, dried apples, rice, salt pork, coffee, and tea), extra clothing, guns and ammunition, and hardware and tools to repair the boats. His scientific equipment included sextants, chronometers, barometers, thermometers, and compasses.

The party consisted of the following people: John Wesley Powell (35 years old); his brother Walter H. Powell (27 years old), who had been a Confederate prisoner during the Civil War and suffered from mental problems; Jack C. Sumner (29 years old), who owned a small Colorado trading post; Oramel G. Howland (35 years old), a part-time editor and printer in Denver; Oramel's brother Seneca B. Howland (25 years old), a Civil War veteran; Bill Dunn (30 years old), a mountaineer; Billy Hawkins (28 years old), a Union army veteran; George Y. Bradley (33 years old), a Union army soldier who agreed to accompany the expedition if Powell could get him out of the army; Frank Goodman, an English adventurer who joined the expedition on a whim; and Andy Hall (about 20 years old), a Scotsman. Powell had selected Sumner, Dunn, Hawkins, and the Howland brothers because of their experience living off the land.

Powell could not pay salaries; the crew members were all volunteers, going along for the adventure. Powell provided only food, weapons, and equipment.

When the men arrived in Green River, they practiced handling the boats and learning Powell's flag and hand signals. They also named their boats. Powell named the pilot boat the *Emma Dean* after his wife. Andy Hall and Billy Hawkins named their boat *Kitty Clyde's Sister*. George Bradley and Walter Powell named theirs the *Maid of the Canyon*. O. G. and Seneca Howland and Frank Goodman could not think of a name, so the other men decided for them: the *No Name*.

On May 24, 1869, the men launched their four boats. They were ready for the adventure of a lifetime! The people of Green River cheered them on.

By May 30, they were in today's Flaming Gorge National Recreation Area. Powell wrote, "We thread the narrow passage with exhilarating velocity, mounting the high waves, whose foaming crests dash over us, and plunging into the troughs, until we reach the quiet water below. Then comes a feeling of great relief. Our first rapid is run."

At first, the men enjoyed the rapids, as people enjoy white-water rafting today. But soon the fun became hard work. The men had to portage the equipment around major rapids and waterfalls. Then the boats either ran through the rapids with no cargo, or the men waded in the cold water, sometimes up to their armpits, to lower each boat by using ropes. This is called lining. In particularly treacherous areas, they took the boats ashore and carried them around the waterfalls.

On June 1, while portaging, they noticed the words "Ashley 1825" painted on a boulder beside the river. Powell named the falls Ashley Falls. Surprisingly, he did not know that in 1825, William H. Ashley went down the Green River looking for beaver.

A week later, Powell spotted danger ahead and signaled the boats to go ashore. He planned to portage their gear around the rapids and line the boats.

Three of the boats went ashore, but O. G. Howland in the *No Name* did not see Powell's signal in time.

The *No Name* swept over the first set of rapids. Out of control, it dropped over a forty-foot waterfall, struck a rock, and dumped the three men into the foaming whirlpool. They grabbed the boat's sides and climbed back in. Two hundred yards farther, the boat plunged through more rapids and slammed into rocks. This time the *No Name* broke into pieces. Amazingly, all three men survived and were rescued.

The next day, Jack Sumner and Andy Hall searched the wreckage. They found a pair of old boots, the barometers, a package of thermometers, and a keg of whiskey. The whiskey had been brought against Powell's orders. Even so, the men cheered when it was found!

They named the area Disaster Falls.

A week later, the men were portaging around another set of rapids. While lowering the *Maid of the Canyon* with ropes, the boat broke loose and plunged through the rapids. Losing another boat would end the expedition, since they could not continue in only two boats. But they were lucky. When the men ran

This illustration, entitled *Wreck at Disaster Falls,* was included in Powell's report on the expedition. In this accident on June 8, 1869, the expedition lost a boat, clothes, three guns, ammunition, blankets, personal belongings, a third of their food, and half of their cooking and eating utensils.

down the riverbank, they found the *Maid of the Canyon* spinning in a whirlpool, unharmed.

The next afternoon, a whirlwind whipped the cook's fire into dry brush near the camp. The fire exploded out of control, and the men ran to the boats. Hawkins scooped up as many cooking utensils as he could carry, but as he climbed into a boat, he tripped. Pots, pans, kettles, bake ovens, plates, knives, forks, and spoons flew through the air and disappeared into the Green River. Bradley suffered burns on his face, neck, and ears, and the fire destroyed much of the men's clothing.

Five weeks into the trip, Powell and a few of the men hiked about thirty miles to the Uinta Indian Agency, where Frank Goodman quit the expedition, saying he had "seen danger enough."

The party was down to nine men and three boats.

On July 8, Powell and George Bradley set off to climb a sheer rock wall that towered six to eight hundred feet above the Green River. Powell suddenly found himself trapped. With his feet in a crevice, he used his one good arm to grab a rock above him. But he could go neither up nor down nor sideways.

He called out to Bradley, who climbed to the rock above Powell. However, he was too high to reach Powell's arm. Bradley looked for a branch or stick for Powell to grab, but there was none.

Powell was balanced on his toes and his muscles shook as he clutched the rock wall. He couldn't remain in that position long, so there was no time to get a rope from the boats.

Then Bradley stripped off his long underwear and lowered them toward Powell. Powell let go of the rock with his only hand and clutched at the dangling pants. Bradley pulled Powell to safety, and the two men continued their climb to the top as if nothing had happened.

On July 11, the party was in the Canyon of Desolation when the major decided to run a difficult set of rapids. It was a bad decision. The *Emma Dean* swamped and flipped over. Jack Sumner and Bill Dunn got the boat through the rapids and to safety, but the party lost two rifles and all of the bedding, and ruined a chronometer. Bradley blamed the major for running the river on Sunday, the Sabbath.

About noon the next day, the crew had already portaged around one rapid when they came to another. Powell in the *Emma Dean* decided to run it instead of portaging, and kept to the left to avoid an overhanging cliff.

The *Emma Dean* got through safely, but the heavy waves carried the *Maid of*

This illustration (which was
included in Powell's report)
shows how George Bradley
took off his "drawers"—his long
underwear!—to rescue Powell
as the two climbed up the side
of a rock.

the Canyon to the right. Bradley was tossed over the side of the boat. As he fell,
his foot got caught. The boat shot through the swift water, dragging him along

head-down in the river. Walter Powell pulled on the oars with all his strength and kept the boat away from the overhanging cliff. Once out of danger, Walter pulled Bradley back into the boat. After that narrow escape, the men lined the *Kitty Clyde's Sister* through the dangerous area.

On the evening of July 16, they reached the junction where the Green and Grand rivers join to become the Colorado River. They made camp for a few days and spread their water-soaked food on rocks to dry. They sifted the lumpy flour through mosquito netting and threw out two hundred pounds that was moldy. They also recaulked and repaired the boats. Powell took measurements and did some exploring. Everyone complained about the noisy crickets.

Back on the river the next morning, the roar of the water became deafening as it crashed against rocks and echoed off the canyon walls. Day after day the men ran so many rapids, they had trouble keeping count. The men were uncomfortable. Water sprayed them all day and wind blew sand over them all night. Thunderstorms soaked them with cold rain. During the day, the temperatures often went above 115 degrees. Their meals consisted mostly of rancid bacon, dried apples, and biscuits made from sour flour. The men were about to starve.

When their oars broke, they made new ones from driftwood. Their clothing never dried. Their shoes were falling apart from constantly wading in water. Insects plagued them, and they were covered with mosquito bites.

The men were eager to get through the canyon. But Major Powell was so absorbed in recording his observations that he ignored the needs of his men.

As the boats came out of Cataract Canyon, a stream poured into the Colorado River from their right. The water was muddy and alkaline. Disgusted with the unpleasant odor, Dunn called it a dirty devil. And Dirty Devil River became the stream's name.

On August 9, the men came to the place where the Little Colorado River flowed into the Colorado River. It was mostly mud and salt. Sumner described it, saying it was "as disgusting a stream as there is on the continent."

The night of August 14, the men slept on rough granite ledges forty to fifty feet above the water. With no room to lie down, they slept sitting up in the rain.

On August 16, the baking soda box accidentally fell into the river. From then on, they had only unleavened bread.

This picture is entitled *Running a Rapid.*

They had no idea how much farther they had to go. The Mormon maps estimated the distance between the Little Colorado and the Grand Wash Cliffs as 70 to 80 miles. Yet they had already run over 120 miles.

On August 26, they discovered a Native American's garden growing beside the river. They landed, stole about a dozen green squashes, and hurried down the river before someone saw them. When they cooked the squashes, Powell wrote, "Never was fruit so sweet as those stolen squashes."

The next day, the river veered to the south, and the rapids seemed worse than any before. Huge boulders clogged the canyon ahead. There was no shore, and no place for the men to stand to line the boats through the rocks. The cliffs that surrounded them were too steep to carry the boats up. Worse, they could see three more treacherous rapids farther downstream.

That evening, O. G. Howland told Powell that he and his brother and Bill Dunn refused to ride the boats any farther. They were quitting the expedition. They would climb out of the canyon and walk to the Mormon settlements.

Powell tried to change O. G.'s mind. He stayed up all night making lunar observations and awoke O. G. in the middle of the night, saying he felt certain they were almost out of the canyon. But the men had made up their minds.

Bradley's journal for August 27 read, "This is decidedly the darkest day of the trip."

The next morning, the party ate breakfast together and launched the boats. Then the three men waved farewell. Those rapids were named Separation Rapids.

With three fewer men, Powell abandoned the *Emma Dean*. The two remaining boats made it through the first set of rapids. That afternoon the *Kitty Clyde's Sister*, with Bradley alone on board, plunged over a waterfall, then disappeared into a whirlpool.

The other five men watched, fearing the worst. Then they saw a dark speck in the foaming water. A moment later the boat emerged, and Bradley waved his hat, signaling that he was okay.

On August 29, the expedition emerged from the Grand Canyon, and the next day they arrived at the mouth of the Virgin River. A Mormon man and his two sons were fishing. They knew about Powell's expedition and were surprised to find Powell alive and safe. They took the men to their fishing cabin and fed them fish and squash. The party ate until, as Bradley wrote, they were "too full for utterance."

When Powell came ashore on August 30, his historic one-hundred-day journey was behind him.

This image of the Grand Canyon is by Solomon Carvalho, who had traveled with John C. Frémont on his fifth expedition.

Four men continued on. Jack Sumner and George Bradley went as far as Fort Yuma in Arizona Territory. Billy Hawkins and Andy Hall ran the last boat all the way to the Gulf of California, arriving in September 1869, and were the first men to negotiate the entire Colorado River.

In Salt Lake City, Powell learned that the three men who climbed out of the canyon—O.G. Howland, Seneca Howland, and Bill Dunn—were killed by a band of Shivwit warriors who mistook them for white miners who had attacked a Shivwit woman.

The men in the expedition had shown outstanding cooperation, teamwork, resourcefulness, and courage. But the trip had not gone as Powell had planned. He had hoped to spend six to nine months mapping the region. Because the river had damaged the instruments, his observations were either incomplete or unreliable. Furthermore, many of his notes had been lost.

The lack of game and other food had turned the trip into a race for survival. The men were more concerned about staying alive than making scientific observations, so Powell did not explore as much as he had planned. Before they came out of the Grand Canyon, Powell knew he would have to repeat the trip.

But the expedition had not been a failure. Powell had determined distances, directions, and the river's course. He had gathered descriptions of rock formations and heights of canyon walls.

When Powell returned to the East, he learned that John A. Risdon had claimed to be the expedition's only survivor. Risdon, who had nothing to do with the venture, had received free train passage to Cheyenne, Wyoming; Omaha, Nebraska; and Springfield, Illinois, as he told a wild story that everyone else had been killed going over a waterfall on May 8. In fact, the expedition hadn't left Green River until May 24.

Newspapers across the country reported Powell's death. Oddly, Risdon's story had an unexpected benefit: The public became *very* interested in the expedition! When Powell returned alive, he was famous and was invited to give lectures around the country. He was an American hero.

Congress appropriated ten thousand dollars for Powell to continue the survey of the region.

Second Expedition: 1871–1872

Powell spent the 1870 summer preparing for another trip. He arranged for supply wagons to meet the boats at prearranged locations. He visited Native American tribes, including the Shivwits, who had killed the Howland brothers and Bill

Dunn. Powell convinced them not to harm his men while they surveyed the plateau.

Three more boats were built in Chicago.

The crew consisted of eleven men: Major John Wesley Powell (37 years old); Frederick S. Dellenbaugh (17 years old), a relative of Powell, assistant topographer, and a self-taught artist; Professor Almon H. Thompson (31 years old), Powell's brother-in-law, chief topographer, astronomer, and geographer; E. O. Beaman, a professional photographer; Francis M. Bishop (28 years old), a topographer; John Steward (30 years old), an amateur geologist; W. C. "Clem" Powell (21 years old), Powell's first cousin; Stephen V. Jones (31 years old), assistant topographer; Frank Richardson, a family friend; Andrew "Andy" Hattan, the cook and handyman; and Jack Hillers, a photographer.

The boats were named the *Canonita*, the *Nellie Powell* (for Nellie Powell Thompson, who was Thompson's wife and the major's sister), and the flagship, a new *Emma Dean*.

On May 22, 1871, the second expedition launched their boats. The whole population of Green River turned out to see them off, but, in Dellenbaugh's words, "that did not make a crowd."

The expedition traveled nine miles down the Green River the first day. That night, Dellenbaugh had a nightmare that some men were stealing the boats. In his sleep, he started strangling Stephen Jones, who was sleeping next to him. Jones yelled and grabbed his gun. Everyone woke up. The men had a good laugh, and Dellenbaugh was extremely embarrassed.

By the third day, the expedition began to get used to running river rapids, wearing wet clothes, and eating unpalatable food.

On June 8, they met some Texans moving a herd of cattle. Frank Richardson had already had enough of river life, and by that point Major Powell had found Richardson unsuitable for the trip. Richardson joined the Texans and rode a mule back to the Green River.

On calm stretches of the river, the men tied the boats together and visited. Powell sat back in his armchair and read to the men from Sir Walter Scott's poem *The Lady of the Lake*. He often read aloud to the men at night beside the campfire.

Powell took no photographic equipment on his first expedition.
But on the second, Jack Hillers and E. O. Beaman both took pictures.
The above image was taken by Hillers. The party is ready to launch their boats in
Green River, Wyoming, May 22, 1871. From left to right: Andrew Hattan, W. C. Powell,
and E. O. Beaman in the *Canonita;* Stephen V. Jones, Jack Hillers, Major Powell, and
Frederick Dellenbaugh in the *Emma Dean*; Professor Almon H. Thompson,
John F. Steward, Francis M. Bishop, and Frank Richardson in the *Nellie Powell.*

Before entering Lodore Canyon, the mosquitoes were terrible, and the
bushes along the river were crawling with snakes. Once in the canyon, they
passed the falls where the *No Name* had wrecked in 1869. They found a sack of
flour, and the cook used it to make biscuits for their dinner.

On the night of June 23, the noise of the roaring river was so loud the men
could not even converse after supper. On July 3, their enemies were ants: They
crawled over everything—even the men's faces while they slept. The next morning, July 4, Fred Dellenbaugh awakened the camp by firing his gun to salute Inde-

Jack Hillers took the above photograph of the first camp on Powell's second expedition. From left to right: Professor Almon H. Thompson, Andrew Hattan, Stephen V. Jones, John F. Steward, W. C. Powell, Frank Richardson, Frederick Dellenbaugh, and Francis M. Bishop.

pendence Day. They celebrated with a meal of ham—a luxury that had been brought along just for this occasion. Dellenbaugh also brought some candy to share from Gunther's in Chicago.

A few days later, Major Powell left the party and traveled to Salt Lake City, leaving Thompson in charge.

The expedition often made camp while various members went on field trips, made scientific observations, took notes on the rocks and topography, and made sketches, charts, and maps.

During this time, Beaman took pictures. Photography was still relatively new, and involved lots of extremely heavy equipment including a camera box, chemical and plate box, and darkroom box. The equipment was carried to a site where a picture was to be taken—five hundred to three thousand feet up the side of a mountain. Then Beaman would set up and begin the lengthy process. Every-

This photograph shows the rapids at Lodore Canyon at the head of Hell's Half Mile. Jones, Hillers, and Dellenbaugh are in the *Emma Dean* at the foot of a rapid.

thing was moved and set up again to take a picture in a different place. It took all afternoon just to take a few pictures.

On July 13, the men were eating breakfast when they heard someone say, "How, how." It was a young brave named Douglas's Boy, the first Native American they had met. He had his bride with him. The men ferried the young couple

On July 13, a young brave named Douglas's Boy and his bride came into camp.
The warrior had stolen his bride from another tribe and they were in hiding.
Jack Hillers took this photograph of a couple that resembled Douglas's Boy and his bride.

and their belongings across the river. Douglas's Boy was fascinated by the "water ponies," but his bride was terrified.

In the middle of the night on July 20, Clem Powell woke up to find Fred Dellenbaugh grasping his leg and saying it was a "big white snake" that was about to bite. The men woke Fred up and had a good laugh. They always took his gun away from him at night, fearing he might shoot them in his sleep.

The second expedition faced different problems from the first expedition. The river was running very low. This was dangerous because the boats often scraped on rocks or gravel on the river bottom, necessitating frequent stops to repair leaks. Also, with a low river, the men had the extra work of portaging around rapids that the 1869 party had been able to run.

On August 5, beavers disturbed the men's sleep with their splashing. Three nights later, in the upper end of the Canyon of Desolation, the party was bothered by bats, and the insects were so loud they called them an insect orchestra and insect opera.

The boats reached Gunnison's Crossing at the end of Gray Canyon on August 25 where Major Powell rejoined them. He brought flour, sugar, jerked beef, overalls, and new shoes for everyone!

As they moved down the river, various members of the party explored ancient Native American villages, finding arrowheads, pieces of pottery, and basket materials. Steward found a complete earthen vessel. They also found fossils and pictographs, and gathered geological and topographical information.

On September 15, they reached the junction where the Grand and Green rivers become the Colorado River. Their meals consisted of three small strips of bacon, a biscuit about the size of a fist, and coffee three times a day. Everyone looked forward to "bean days."

As they entered Cataract Canyon, the letdowns through the rapids were extremely difficult. The men could barely keep their balance on the slick rocks while holding the boats. The work was even more difficult since the paint on the boats' bottoms had been scraped by rocks and gravel. After four months on the river, the wood had become water-saturated, making the boats extremely heavy to lift over or around boulders.

When they arrived at the Dirty Devil River, they cached the *Canonita* so that it would be available the following year. Powell had arranged for a pack train to meet them with supplies, but it didn't arrive, and the men faced another hundred miles of river with the already-low rations.

When they reached El Vado de los Padres (the Crossing of the Fathers), they spotted the second pack train's little white flag. Spirits soared with the arrival of fresh food, strong overalls, heavy work shoes, and mail for everyone.

But health problems plagued the party. On September 18, Stephen Jones seriously injured his leg while boarding a boat. Jones also had rheumatism in his knees. Bishop had been shot in the chest during the Civil War and now suffered from pleurisy and had difficulty breathing. Steward was also ill. He ran high fevers and was in so much pain he could not get up for over a week.

On the morning of September 29, Andy Hattan forgot to turn his shoe upside down before putting it on. A scorpion had crawled into the shoe during the night, and it stung him. The sting continued to pain Hattan, and made him pale and thin.

On October 10, Major Powell again left the expedition and returned to Salt Lake City, leaving Thompson in charge.

As the expedition prepared to move down the river, some friendly Navajos came into camp. When the party began boarding the boats, the Navajos shook hands with the men and then sat on the riverbank watching.

The expedition reached the mouth of the Paria River on October 23. That evening, nine Navajo men and four Mormons joined them. They spent a great evening around the campfire. The Navajos sang and chanted; the Mormons sang their songs. Then as the chief paddled on a camp kettle, everyone joined hands and laughed at one another while they danced around the campfire to a war song.

The expedition had completed the first portion of the journey. The two boats were cached, and the men climbed out of the canyon to the plateau to begin surveying.

Jones and Steward were so ill that they were taken to the village of Kanab. Both men recovered from their illnesses, but Steward never returned to the expedition.

The rest of the party set up camp. Immediately, they had problems with wolves. Wolves stole a portion of beef hanging from a high tree limb, a ham, and two large sacks of jerked beef from near the men's heads. The wolves ate anything leather and anything containing grease.

Powell rejoined the party in December and brought his wife and three-month-old daughter. Thompson's wife and her dog, Fuzz, came along, too. Pow-

The above photo shows Jack Hillers developing his photographs
in camp on the Aquarius Plateau over the 1871–1872 winter.

ell and his family left the following February and went to Washington, D.C., to request more money from Congress.

The party continued the surveying work and making topographical maps despite the cold, snow, and wind. In June 1872, Thompson and Dellenbaugh discovered the last uncharted river in the West. They named it the Escalante River after Father Silvestre Velez de Escalante, who had explored the region in 1776. They also recorded a mountain range not shown on the maps and named it the Henry Mountains.

In August, Powell rejoined the party to finish the survey by boat. There were only seven men left: Major Powell, Clem Powell, Fred Dellenbaugh, Stephen Jones, Andy Hattan, Almon Thompson, and Jack Hillers.

The expedition left from Lees Ferry on August 17, 1872, in the *Emma Dean* and the *Canonita*, which an exploring party had retrieved in June. They abandoned the *Nellie Powell* because it was in poor condition.

In 1871, the river had been very low, but heavy winter snows and spring rains in 1872 had raised the water to a higher-than-normal level.

As the party started through Marble Canyon, the rock walls were 200 feet high. By afternoon they were 700 feet high, and by the following afternoon they were 1,200 feet high on both sides. Each day they descended deeper in the canyon, and the walls towered above them 2,500 feet, then 3,000 feet, then 3,500 feet.

The boats plunged through rapid after rapid—twelve on August 20, ten the next day, seventeen the next. On August 22, they passed the mouth of the Little Colorado. The rapids were so close together that at one point Major Powell yelled above the roar of the water, "By God, boys, we're gone."

But they weren't gone. The river took command of the boats, and after a harrowing, unbelievable ride, they made it through what Dellenbaugh described as "seething, boiling turmoil!"

They entered the Grand Canyon on August 24, and even going ashore was hazardous because of Gila monsters, tarantulas, scorpions, and rattlesnakes. When they made camp that night, they were 6,500 feet—a mile and a quarter—down in the canyon. They remained in camp for three days, taking measurements and making geological notes.

On August 28, Jack Hillers injured his back lifting the *Canonita* over a rock.

The exploring party returned to the mouth of the Dirty Devil River in June 1872 to retrieve the boat that was cached in 1871. The *Canonita* was in good condition. Above, the men are doing routine maintenance work. Left to right: W. Johnson (who worked with the party for a short time while they surveyed), Frederick Dellenbaugh, and Jack Hillers. This photograph was taken by James Fennemore.

The pain completely disabled him and he could hardly move for twenty-four hours.

The next day, they pulled ashore near noon and stepped out of the boats to look at a tremendous waterfall in the river ahead. On each side of them, solid granite walls soared a thousand feet high, straight up out of the water. With no

This photograph was taken on the Colorado River looking upstream in Marble Canyon.
Powell's armchair was strapped to the center compartment of the *Emma Dean* to
give him a better view of the canyons. His life preserver is on the floor of the boat,
behind the chair. Since Powell had only one arm and could not swim,
he used his life preserver often on both expeditions.

shoreline, a portage or letdown was impossible. There was nothing to do but ride
the boats down the waterfall.

The *Emma Dean* went first with Dellenbaugh, Jones, Hillers, and the major.
Waves broke over the boat and created a canopy of foam over the men's heads.
The boat shot through the current, leaping out of the water and then lunging into
it. Amazingly, it didn't crash on any of the enormous boulders.

Then Clem Powell, Hattan, and Thompson descended the waterfall in the
Canonita. They also avoided damage to the boat.

This photo shows the men repairing one of the boats at First Granite Gorge
on the Colorado River in the Grand Canyon.

A few hours later, they reached another treacherous waterfall. Using ropes, they lowered the boats partway down. When darkness and a heavy rain overtook them, they spent the night sleeping on the rocks.

The next morning, as they continued lowering the boats in the rain, rocks gouged holes in the bottoms, so the men began making repairs. But as they worked, they realized the river was rising rapidly—three feet an hour. They raised the boats another six feet and secured them with ropes to the side of the cliff so that one group of men could continue the repairs.

The other group began moving their gear, food, and equipment up the side of the sheer cliff. Everything was soaked. Some of the men climbed to a ledge about thirty or forty feet above the water. The others passed the gear up the side of the rock wall.

The group repairing the boats finished their work and lined the boats up to a place where they hoped to be safe from the rising river. Clem Powell wrote in his journal that if the boats "go—God help us. 'Tis an anxious night for us all."

They spent the night of August 30 sleeping on the hard granite ledges above the roaring river.

The next morning, the river had risen even more. As they launched the *Emma Dean,* they accidentally stove a hole in her side, but they had to take a chance on running the next rapid with water gushing in through the hole.

Amazingly, both boats made it through the waterfall. They landed and made repairs. Late that afternoon, they negotiated eight heavy rapids in one hour. At one point, Thompson tumbled overboard while going through a rapid, but he climbed right back into the boat. Jones wrote that it was "the most exciting ride of my life."

The river was running at least ten feet higher than it had been on Powell's 1869 expedition. The power of the rushing water shook the earth.

On September 3, the *Emma Dean* plunged over a waterfall and turned upside down, throwing all four men out. Almost immediately, a whirlpool sucked Jack

Hillers and the major under the water. It tore off Jack's shoes and socks. The major was wearing his life jacket, and it saved his life.

Jones and Dellenbaugh managed to pull the boat upright and all four climbed back in. They lost kettles, an ax, an oar, and some small items. The major's five-hundred-dollar chronometer was ruined. Their bailing kettles had swept away, but amazingly their hats had remained on their heads.

The *Canonita* was not as heavily loaded as the *Emma Dean*, and it came through the waterfall losing only one oar and breaking an oarlock.

This section of the river is now known as Serpentine Falls.

A few hours later, the *Emma Dean* got turned around in swift water at the head of a rapid and was drifting stern-first. Dellenbaugh grabbed a rope, but as he jumped to a rock, the boat lurched and pulled him into the water.

The major reached out to catch Dellenbaugh, but he was too far away. Stephen Jones also tried, but he slipped and fell, skinning his shins.

Dellenbaugh clung to the rope, and the current towed him downstream. When the boat turned into a huge wave, Dellenbaugh climbed inside and steered it safely into an eddy.

They covered almost nine miles that day and ran sixteen rapids—most of them difficult.

The next morning, the boats had to be patched before continuing downstream. The canyon walls towered 4,000 feet above them. That day they ran 23 rapids in 14 miles.

By September 6, things had improved a little, but the next day they ran what Jones called "one of the worst rapids on the trip."

On the evening of September 7, they arrived at the mouth of Kanab Creek. The pack train with supplies was there to meet them, but they brought bad news. The Utes were on the warpath, and the Shivwits were planning to attack Powell's party.

On the morning of September 9, Powell made an announcement. "Well, boys," he said, "our voyage is done." They were only halfway through the Grand

The above photograph was taken from the top of the Grand Canyon by Jack Hillers
after the end of Powell's second expedition.

Canyon, but he had decided to end the expedition. The exhausted men were both pleased and disappointed .

Though the second expedition was ended early, it brought back excellent topographic maps, geological information about the Grand Canyon, Powell's

Major John Wesley Powell (right) is dressed in a native costume. He is shown with Tau-ruv, a member of the Paiute tribe. The photo was taken in Uinta Valley. The Utes and Shoshones gave Powell the name Ka-pu-rats, meaning "One Arm Off."

Major Powell is shown in the above photo in a conference with a group of Utes. Powell trusted the tribes, so they trusted him. Because of Powell's remarkable ability to win the Native Americans' trust, he was able to document their lives and customs.

account of the expedition, the diaries of six of the men, and hundreds of photographs.

Oddly, when Powell wrote the report of his expeditions, he mixed the details of the two, so the report reads as though there was only one trip down the Green and Colorado rivers. Through the journals of the other men, historians have traced on which expedition the various events occurred.

In 1878, Powell wrote an extremely important book about the western United States. Entitled *Report on the Land of the Arid Regions of the United States*, it included the characteristics of the land and the amount of rainfall. Powell suggested the land be classified as to how it could best be used—farming, mining, grazing, or lumbering. He recommended that water be conserved and managed with irrigation projects, reservoirs, and damming of rivers. Powell's water management policies made cattlemen, land developers, and politicians angry. But history proved he was right. Powell was one of America's earliest conservationists.

Powell helped establish the U.S. Geological Survey, which combined his own work with the surveys of Clarence King, George Wheeler, and F. V. Hayden. Clarence King served as the agency's first director, but he quit after a year. Powell then served as director from 1881 to 1894.

Powell also compiled information about the Native Americans, including their languages, habits and customs, religious beliefs, history, tribal structure, and mythology. After reading Powell's study of the Native Americans and their cultures, Congress created the United States Bureau of Ethnology in 1879. Powell was the first director and he held that position until his death.

For many years, he was the director of two bureaus at the same time.

Powell died on September 23, 1902, in Haven, Maine. Before he died, John Wesley Powell and a colleague made a bet on which man's brain was larger. Each man included in his will a provision that his brain should be removed at his death. A doctor compared the two brains and Powell won the bet. Powell's brain is still in the collection of the Smithsonian Institution.

THE EXPLORATION CONTINUES

When John Wesley Powell explored the Green and Colorado rivers, he was essentially exploring the last unmapped, uncharted, and unexplored region of the United States.

But that doesn't mean there's nothing left to discover.

As recently as 1974, two American adventurers made an amazing discovery in southern Arizona when they found an underground cavern previously unknown to modern man. Randy Tufts and Gary Tenen knew the caverns they had discovered were extraordinary, and they kept them a secret to protect the area from vandals and improper preservation. They didn't even tell the people who owned the land, the Kartchners, until 1978.

Now named the Kartchner Caverns, the 250,000-year-old cave is one of the most spectacular in the world. It is a "wet" or "living" cave, which means its stalactites and stalagmites are still forming. It has two main rooms that are both the size of football fields, with ceilings one hundred feet high.

In 1988, the Arizona State Parks purchased the site and opened it to the public. The spectacular caverns are constantly monitored to safeguard the temperatures and humidity inside, as well as to protect the fragile environment from human destruction.

While the Kartchner Caverns are a modern discovery in the United States, at this very moment explorers are poking around in remote corners of planet Earth. Their discoveries have been phenomenal—the source of the Amazon River, ancient ruins in Peru's rain forests, the lost city of Conturmarca in Peru, Incan mummies in an Andean volcano, Phoenician ships, and the Shangri-La waterfall in Tibet, to name a few.

Oceanographers have only begun to explore Earth's oceans. About 71 percent of the planet's surface is covered by oceans, and only about 5 percent has been explored.

Besides exploring the ocean floor, there are also underwater shipwrecks to find. And there are still amazing discoveries on land—previously unknown waterfalls and caves, as well as jungles, deserts, and mountain ranges around the world. There are ancient tribes, buried cities, and dinosaurs to dig up, and lost treasures yet to find.

And, of course, there's an entire universe for space explorers.

In fact, there are so many people out exploring that they even have their own club—the Explorers Club. In the 1700s and 1800s, few women went exploring. Thankfully, times have changed, as reflected in the membership of the Explorers Club.

For anyone who can know the dangers but face them willingly, who can accept risk in the pursuit of knowledge, who has the same sense of adventure that the explorers in this book had . . . the world, and the universe, awaits!

Notes

Chapter 1

p. 15: "sham sale," "merely to . . . troubles." Frederic W. Howay, ed., *Voyages of the "Columbia" to the Northwest Coast 1787–1790 and 1790–1793* (Boston: The Massachusetts Historical Society, 1941), 471.

p. 17: "This fine . . . destroy'd." Ibid., 391.

p. 17: That Gray burned the Nootkan village because the tribe refused to trade with him was found in Dan L. Thrapp's *Encyclopedia of Frontier Biography* (Lincoln, Nebr.: University of Nebraska Press, 1988), 583.

p. 17: That Vancouver's destination was the Strait of Juan de Fuca was found in several places: W. Kaye Lamb, ed., *Dictionary of Canadian Biography*, vol. 4 (Toronto: University of Toronto Press, 1979), 745; and John M. Naish's *The Mariner's Mirror*, vol. 80, no. 4 (November 1994), 421; and Frederic W. Howay, ed., *Voyages of the "Columbia" to the Northwest Coast 1787–1790 and 1790–1793*, 336.

p. 18: "[F]ifty four . . . plates." Ibid., 411.

p. 19: "*Ne plus ultra*," "I am . . . man!" Bern Anderson, *Surveyor of the Sea: The Life and Voyages of Capt. George Vancouver* (Seattle: University of Washington Press, 1960), 13.

p. 21: Details of Vancouver's assignment were found in several places: W. Kaye Lamb, ed., *Dictionary of Canadian Biography*, 745; John M. Naish's *The Interwoven Lives of George Vancouver, Archibald Mensizes, Joseph Whidbey and Peter Puget* (London: The Edwin Mellen Press, 1996), 87; and W. Kaye Lamb, ed., *The Voyage of George Vancouver, 1791–1795*, Vol. 1 (London: The Hakluyt Society, 1984), 40.

p. 21: Details pertaining to Vancouver's fireworks display were found in W. Kaye Lamb, ed., *George Vancouver: A Voyage of Discovery to the North Pacific Ocean and Round the World 1791–1795*, vol. 3 (London: The Hakluyt Society, 1984), 1200.

p. 21: "the river colored water" and "streams . . . bay." W. Kaye Lamb, ed., *George Vancouver: A Voyage of Discovery to the North Pacific Ocean and Round the World 1791–1795*, vol. 2 (London: The Hakluyt Society, 1984), 497.

p. 23: "Poo Poo." John M. Naish, *The Interwoven Lives of George Vancouver, Archibald Mensizes, Joseph Whidbey and Peter Puget*, 151.

p. 24: "situation . . . degree." W. Kaye Lamb, ed., *George Vancouver: A Voyage of Discovery to the North Pacific*

Ocean and Round the World
1791–1795, vol. 2, 641.

p. 27: "vixen," "a remarkably . . . ornament."
W. Kaye Lamb, ed., *George Vancouver:
A Voyage of Discovery to the North
Pacific Ocean and Round the World
1791–1795*, vol. 3, 1054.

p. 27: "three . . . cheers," "an additional . . .
occasion." W. Kaye Lamb, ed., *George
Vancouver: A Voyage of Discovery to
the North Pacific Ocean and Round
the World 1791–1795*, vol. 4 (London:
The Hakluyt Society, 1984), 1371.

p. 28: "carried on . . . Exchange." Bern
Anderson, ed., "Notes and Documents:
The Vancouver Expedition: Peter
Puget's Journal of the Exploration of
Puget Sound, May 7–June 11, 1792,"
Pacific Northwest Quarterly 30
(April 1939): 213.

p. 29: "Alexander Mackenzie . . . ninety-
three." W. Kaye Lamb, ed., *Dictionary
of Canadian Biography*, 540; W. Kaye
Lamb, ed., *The Journals and Letters of
Sir Alexander Mackenzie (Voyages
From Montreal, on the River St.
Laurence, through the Continent)*
(London: Cambridge University
Press, 1970), 378; and James K. Smith,
Alexander Mackenzie, Explorer
(Toronto: McGraw-Hill Ryerson
Limited, 1973), 113.

p. 33: "[W]ithout . . . succeeding." W. Kaye
Lamb, ed., *The Journals and Letters of
Sir Alexander Mackenzie*, 450.

p. 33: Details of the canoe's packing as well
as "our dog" were found in two
sources: James K. Smith, *Alexander
Mackenzie, Explorer*, 90; and Bary
Gough, *First Across the Continent:
Sir Alexander Mackenzie* (Norman,
Okla.: University of Oklahoma
Press, 1997), 123.

pp. 34, 39 and 40: Frances Anne Hopkins
painted *Canoe Party Around
Campfire* and *Voyageurs at Dawn*.
Mrs. Hopkins was an English amateur
painter married to the governor of the
Hudson's Bay Company. She traveled
with her husband and painted many
scenes. The only women who traveled
on Alexander Mackenzie's voyages
were Native American women.

p. 38: That the Indians sobbed and wept was
found in several sources: Bary Gough,
*First Across the Continent: Sir
Alexander Mackenzie*, 132; Ogden
Tanner, *The Old West Series: The
Canadians* (Alexandia, Va.: Time-Life
Books, 1977), 60; and Roy Daniells,
*Alexander Mackenzie and the North
West* (New York: Barnes and Noble,
Inc., 1969), 126.

p. 39: (Caption) That the gum substance
made the canoe very heavy to carry
was found in W. Kaye Lamb, ed., *The
Journals and Letters of Sir Alexander
Mackenzie*, 302.

p. 40: "the weather . . . experienced." W.
Kaye Lamb, ed., *The Journals and Letters of Sir Alexander Mackenzie*, 358.

p. 41: The incident with Mackenzie's stolen
ax was found in Bary Gough, *First
Across the Continent: Sir Alexander*

Mackenzie, 147; and W. Kaye Lamb, ed., *The Journals and Letters of Sir Alexander Mackenzie*, 370.

p. 41: The fact that "our dog" had gone missing was found in Ibid., 372; and Bary Gough, *First Across the Continent: Sir Alexander Mackenzie*, 158.

p. 41: That "Macunah"—or Vancouver—had fired at the Indians was found in several sources: Roy Daniells, *Alexander Mackenzie and the North West*, 151-152; W. Kaye Lamb, ed., *The Journals and Letters of Sir Alexander Mackenzie*, 381; and Bary Gough, *First Across the Continent: Sir Alexander Mackenzie*, 150-151.

Chapter 2

p.48: "good hunter . . . degree." Reuben Gold Thwaites, LL.D., ed., *Original Journals of the Lewis and Clark Expedition 1804-1806*, vol. 7 (New York: Dodd, Mead, 1905), 227.

p. 52: "Colter, I . . . wounded." John Bradbury, F.L.S., *Travels in the Interior of America in the Years 1809, 1810, and 1811* (Liverpool and London: Sherwood, Neely, and Jones, 1817), 18.

p. 52: "he was . . . of." Ibid., 19.

pp. 52–54: There are several versions of Colter's escape from the Blackfeet in 1808. This book generally uses the following version: General Thomas James, *Three Years Among the Mexicans and the Indians* (Chicago: The

Rio Grande Press, 1846, 1902; reprint, St. Louis Historical Society of Missouri, 1962), 57–65.

p. 54: "If God . . . again!" Ibid., 65.

p. 58: "no trivial . . . voyage." Zebulon Montgomery Pike, *Exploratory Travels Through the Western Territories of North America: Comprising A Voyage from St. Louis, on the Mississippi, to the Source of that River, and a Journey Through the Interior of Louisiana and the North-Eastern Provinces of New Spain* (London: Paternoster-Row, 1811; reprint, Denver: W. H. Lawrence & Co., 1889), 86.

p. 59: "prevent alarm or offence." W. Eugene Hollon, *The Lost Pathfinder: Zebulon Montgomery Pike* (Norman, Okla.: University of Oklahoma Press, 1949), 101.

p. 62: "I believe . . . summit." Zebulon Montgomery Pike, *Exploratory Travels Through the Western Territories of North America*, 208.

p. 63: "This was . . . miserably." Ibid., 220, 221.

p. 64: "What, is . . . River?" "No, sir . . . Norte." Ibid., 237.

p. 65: "heaven-like . . . kindness." Ibid., 313.

p. 65: That Pike pretended to be lost was found in several sources: Daniel Baker, *Explorers and Discoverers of the World* (Detroit, Mich.: Gale Research, Inc., 1993), 446; Donald Jackson, "How Lost was Zebulon Pike?" *American Heritage* 16, no. 2 (February 1965), 14; and W. Eugene

Hollon, *The Lost Pathfinder: Zebulon Montgomery Pike* (Norman, Okla.: University of Oklahoma Press, 1949), 141.

p. 66: (caption) "Push on ... fellows." W. Eugene Hollon, *The Lost Pathfinder: Zebulon Montgomery Pike*, 213.

p. 67: "White man ... boat." Reuben Gold Thwaites, ed., "Account of an Expedition From Pittsburgh To the Rocky Mountains, Performed in the Years 1819, 1820," compiled by Edwin James, *Early Western Travels 1748–1846*, vol. 14 (Cleveland: The Arthur H. Clark Co., 1905), 178.

p. 71: The list of expedition members that set off with Long in 1820 was found in Roger L. Nichols and Patrick L. Halley, *Stephen Long and American Frontier Exploration* (Norman, Okla.: University of Oklahoma Press, 1995), 120.

p. 72: "You must ... heavens." Reuben Gold Thwaites, ed., "Account of an Expedition From Pittsburgh To the Rocky Mountains, Performed in the Years 1819, 1820," compiled by Edwin James, *Early Western Travels 1748–1846*, vol. 15 (Cleveland: The Arthur H. Clark Co., 1905), 206.

pp. 73: "Your heart ... protector." Ibid., 211.

pp. 74: Like Pike and many other western explorers (including John C. Frémont), these explorers did not anticipate the difficulty of the climb when they set out to scale the mountain now known as Pikes Peak. They underestimated the time that would be required and the amount of food they should carry along. This is still a common problem in the Rocky Mountains. Today, rescue parties often have to search for inexperienced hikers who underestimate the difficulty of a climb.

p. 74: "intolerable." Harlin M. Fuller and LeRoy R. Hafen, eds., *The Far West and the Rockies Historical Series 1820–1875 The Journal of Captain John R. Bell* (Glendale, Calif.: The Arthur H. Clark Company, 1957), 164.

p. 76: That the Osage were indignant was found in Harlin M. Fuller and LeRoy R. Hafen, eds., *The Far West and the Rockies Historical Series 1820–1875 The Journal of Captain John R. Bell*, 261.

p. 78: That Long must have been mortified was found in Edwin James, *Account of an Expedition from Pittsburgh to the Rocky Mountains*, vol. 2 (Ann Arbor, Mich.: University Microfilms, Inc., 1966), 167.

p. 79: "In regard ... country." Reuben Gold Thwaites, ed., "Account of an Expedition From Pittsburgh To the Rocky Mountains, Performed in the Years 1819, 1820," compiled by Edwin James, *Early Western Travels 1748–1846*, vol. 15, 147.

Chapter 3

p. 85: (ad) "To Enterprising Young Men."

Richard M. Clokey, *William H. Ashely: Enterprise and Politics in the Trans-Mississippi West* (Norman, Okla.: University of Oklahoma Press, 1980), 67

p. 89: "peetrified trees . . . songs," "peetrified bushes." Dee Brown, *The Best of Dee Brown's West: An Anthology* (Santa Fe: Clear Light Publishers, 1998), 125; Stanley Vestal, *Jim Bridger: Mountain Man* (New York: William Morrow and Co., 1946), 210; and J. Cecil Alter, *James Bridger: Trapper, Frontiersman, Scout and Guide* (Salt Lake City, Utah: Shepard Book Company, 1925), 383.

p. 89: Bridger's story ending with "Why, the Injun killed me!" was found in J. Lee Humfreville's *Twenty Years among our Hostile Indians* (New York, Hunter and Co., 1899), 466.

p. 91: There are many versions of Hugh Glass's survival story. This version is adapted from Stanley Vestal, *Jim Bridger, Mountain Man* (New York: William Morrow, 1946), 40–56.

p. 100: The list of languages spoken by Bridger was found in Ibid., 207.

p. 100: "The whole . . . see it." Maj. Gen. Grenville M. Dodge, *Biographical Sketch of James Bridger, Mountaineer, Trapper and Guide* (New York: Unz and Company, 1905), 26.

p. 101: "No such . . . lived," "infernal lies." J. Lee Humfreville, *Twenty Years Among Our Hostile Indians*, 467–468.

p. 106: "O you . . . other." Charles L. Camp, *James Clyman, Frontiersman* (Portland, Oreg.: Champoeg Press, 1960), 18.

p. 112: "perish in . . . unpitied." Maurice S. Sullivan, *The Travels of Jedediah Smith: A Documentary Outline Including the Journal of the Great American Pathfinder* (Lincoln, Nebr.: University of Nebraska Press, 1934, 1961), 21.

pp. 113–118: In the massacres of 1827 and 1828, Smith was the leader of the expeditions in which 25 of his men were killed. All of the men were like brothers, and the deaths were extremely difficult for Smith. So why did these massacres occur?

Native Americans would have wanted the men's weapons and horses.

Furthermore, Smith's small group of men was far outnumbered in both situations.

In a letter from Jedediah Smith and his two partners to General William Clark, Superintendent of Indian Affairs, they blame "British interlopers," meaning the British fur traders, who were influencing the Native Americans and prejudicing the tribes against the Americans.

There are those who suggest Smith was too careless, too willing to take chances, overconfident, too trusting, used bad judgment, or let his guard down. Some say it was simply a matter of bad luck.

It would be wrong to place blame using twenty-first-century standards. Smith lived in different times and under circumstances hardly imaginable today. Even in 1828, there could be no single answer.

p. 115: "head foremost." Dale L. Morgan, *Jedediah Smith and the Opening of the West* (Lincoln, Nebr.: University of Nebraska Press, 1953), 260.

p. 115: "moody silence of hunger." Maurice S. Sullivan, *The Travels of Jedediah Smith*, 98.

p. 120: "I kept . . . Walker." Joel P. Walker, *A Pioneer of Pioneers: Narrative of Adventures Thro' Alabama, Florida, New Mexico, Oregon, California, & C.* (Los Angeles: Glen Dawson, 1953), 7.

p. 121: "Mr. Walker . . . delight." John C. Ewers, ed., *Adventures of Zenas Leonard* (Norman, Okla.: University of Oklahoma Press, 1959), 64.

p. 123: "the extreme . . . west." Ibid., 89.

p. 123: The dried fish incident was written about in Bil Gilbert's *Westering Man: The Life of Joseph Walker* (New York: Atheneum, 1983) 133.

p. 127: "presented a . . . spectacle." John C. Ewers, ed., *Adventures of Zenas Leonard*, 128.

p. 128: "[I'm going . . . mean." Bil Gilbert, *Westering Man: The Life of Joseph Walker*, 43.

p. 129: "the most . . . knew." Ibid, 215.

Chapter 4

p. 133: "manifest destiny . . . millions." Howard R. Lamar, ed., *The New Encyclopedia of the American West* (New Haven: Yale University Press, 1998), 676.

p. 137: Description of Nicollet and Frémont mapping expedition of the upper Mississippi and Missouri Rivers: Bil Gilbert, *The Trailblazers* (Alexandria, Va.: Time-Life Books, 1973), 156.

p. 141: Altitude sickness is common in areas high above sea level. Because there is less oxygen in the atmosphere, the lack of oxygen can cause dizziness, headache, impaired judgment, vomiting, nosebleeds, weakness, fatigue, lightheadedness, and even unconsciousness. Frémont experienced altitude sickness on his first and fourth expeditions.

p. 144: When John C. Frémont reached Fort Vancouver, in present-day Washington State, it was controlled by the British Hudson's Bay Company. Dr. John McLoughlin, who was in charge of the fort, was a physician as well as a fur trader. He was generally kind as well as powerful, both physically and businesswise: he held control over the fur trade in the Northwest from 1824 to 1845. McLoughlin had extended kindness to Jedediah Smith in 1828 after 14 of Smith's men were massacred.

p. 145: "remote, desolate land" and the

brandy toast on Christmas day were documented in Ferol Egan's *Fremont, Explorer for a Restless Nation* (Garden City, N.Y.: Doubleday & Co., Inc., 1977), 188.

p. 148: "suffering from lightheadedness," "deranged." Ibid., 216.

p. 149: That Kit Carson and Alexis Godey returned with scalps and stolen horses was found in Ibid., 242.

p. 149: That the dog was happy to see Pablo was found in Ibid., 244.

p. 159: (menu, caption) Thos. E. Breckenridge, as told to J. W. Freeman and Charles W. Watson, "The Story of a Famous Expedition," *Cosmopolitan Magazine*, August 1896, 403–404.

p. 161: (caption) "We awoke . . . fire." Ibid., 403.

Chapter 5

pp. 172–173: "We thread . . . run." J. W. Powell, *The Exploration of the Colorado River and Its Canyons* (New York: Dover Publications, 1961), 134.

p. 177: "as disgusting . . . continent." William Culp Darrah, ed., "J. C. Sumner's Journal," *Utah Historical Quarterly* 15 (1947), 119.

p. 179: "Never was . . . squashes." Powell, 275.

p. 179: "This is . . . trip." William Culp Darrah, ed., "George Y. Bradley's Journal," *Utah Historical Quarterly,* 15 (1947), 70.

p. 179: "too full . . . utterance." Ibid., 72.

p. 182: "that did . . . crowd." Frederick S. Dellenbaugh, *A Canyon Voyage: The Narrative of the Second Powell Expedition Down the Green-Colorado River from Wyoming, and the Explorations on Land, in the Years 1871 and 1872* (New Haven: Yale University Press, 1926), 9.

p. 187: "water ponies." Richard A. Bartlett, *Great Surveys of the American West* (Norman, Okla.: University of Oklahoma Press, 1962), 288.

p. 187: "big white snake." Journal of Walter Clement Powell (*Utah Historical Quarterly* vol. 16-17), 288.

p. 190: "By God . . . gone." Frederick S. Dellenbaugh, *A Canyon Voyage*, 221.

p. 190: "seething . . . turmoil!" Ibid.

p. 194: "go— . . . all.": Charles Kelly, ed., "Journal of W. C. Powell," *Utah Historical Quarterly* 16–17 (1948–1949), 444.

p. 194: "the most . . . life." Dr. Herbert E. Gregory, ed., "Journal of Stephen Vindiver Jones," *Utah Historical Quarterly* 16–17 (1948–1949), 150.

p. 195: "one of . . . trip." Ibid., 153.

p. 195: "Well, boys . . . done." Frederick S. Dellenbaugh, *A Canyon Voyage*, 242.

SELECTED BIBLIOGRAPHY

General

Cleland, Robert Glass. *This Reckless Breed of Men: The Trappers and Fur Traders of the Southwest.* New York: Alfred A. Knopf, 1950.

Goetzmann, William H. *Exploration and Empire: The Explorer and the Scientist in the Winning of the American West.* New York: Alfred A. Knopf, 1966.

Lamar, Howard R., ed. *The New Encyclopedia of the American West.* New Haven: Yale University Press, 1998.

Thrapp, Dan L. *Encyclopedia of Frontier Biography.* Lincoln, Nebr.: University of Nebraska Press, 1988.

Bridger, James

Alter, J. Cecil. *Jim Bridger.* Norman, Okla.: University of Oklahoma Press, 1925, 1950, 1962.

Brown, D. Alexander. "Jim Bridger." *American History Illustrated* 3, no. 4 (July 1968): 4–11, 44–47.

Dodge, Maj. Gen. Grenville M. *Biographical Sketch of James Bridger: Mountaineer, Trapper and Guide.* New York: Unz and Company, 1905.

Gowans, Fred R., and Eugene E. Campbell. *Fort Bridger: Island in the Wilderness.* Provo, Utah: Brigham

Young University Press, 1975.

Humfrevllle, J. Lee. *Twenty Years Among Our Hostile Indians.* New York: Hunter and Co., 1899.

Ismert, Cornelius M. "James Bridger." *The Mountain Men and the Fur Trade of the Far West,* vol. 6. Edited by LeRoy R. Hafen. Glendale, Calif.: The Arthur H. Clark Co., 1968.

Spence, Clark C. "A Celtic Nimrod in the Old West." *Montana: The Magazine of Western History* 9, no. 2 (spring 1959): 56–66.

Stansbury, Captain Howard. *Exploration and Survey of the Valley of the Great Salt Lake of Utah.* Philadelphia: Lippincott, Grambo and Co., 1852.

Vestal, Stanley. *Jim Bridger, Mountain Man.* New York: William Morrow, 1946.

Colter, John

Bradbury, John, F.L.S. *Travels in the Interior of America in the Years 1809, 1810, and 1811.* Liverpool and London: Sherwood, Neely, and Jones, 1817.

Ghent, W. J. "A Sketch of John Colter." *Wyoming Annals* 10, no. 3 (July 1938): 111–116.

Haines, Aubrey L. "John Colter." *The Mountain Man and the Fur Trade of the Far West,* vol. 8. Edited by LeRoy

R. Hafen. Glendale, Calif.: The Arthur H. Clark Co., 1971.

Harris, Burton. *John Colter: His Years in the Rockies*. New York: Charles Scribner's Sons, 1952.

James, General Thomas. *Three Years Among the Mexicans and the Indians*. Chicago: The Rio Grande Press, 1846, 1902. Reprint, St. Louis: The Historical Society of Missouri, 1962.

Oglesby, Richard Edward. *Manuel Lisa and the Opening of the Missouri Fur Trade*. Norman, Okla.: University of Oklahoma Press, 1963.

Vinton, Stallo. *John Colter, Discoverer of Yellowstone Park: An Account of His Exploration in 1807 and of His Further Adventures As Hunter, Trapper, Indian Fighter, Pathfinder and Member of the Lewis and Clark Expedition*. New York: Edward Eberstadt, 1926.

Exploration Continues

O'Neill, Helen (Associated Press), "Modern Explorers Still Discover Wild Places," (Colo.) *Boulder Daily Camera*, 20 May 2000, sec. C, p. 7.

(untitled press release) Phoenix: Arizona State Parks, 1999.

Frémont, John Charles

Brandon, William. *The Men and the Mountain: Frémont's Fourth Expedition*. New York: William Morrow, 1955.

Breckenridge, Thos. E., as told to J. W. Freeman and Charles W. Watson. "The Story of a Famous Expedition." *Cosmopolitan Magazine*, (August 1896): 400–408.

Egan, Ferol. *Frémont: Explorer for a Restless Nation*. Garden City, N. Y.: Doubleday, 1977.

Frémont, Brevet Col. J. C. *The Exploration Expedition to the Rocky Mountains, Oregon and California to Which Is Added a Description of the Physical Geography of California With Recent Notices of the Gold Region from the Latest and Most Authentic Sources*. Buffalo, N.Y.: Geo. H. Derby & Co, 1850.

Goetzmann, William H. *Army Exploration in the American West 1803–1863*. New Haven: Yale University Press, 1959.

Hafen, LeRoy R., and Ann W. Hafen, eds. *Frémont's Fourth Expedition: A Documentary Account of the Disaster of 1848–1849 with Diaries, Letters, and Reports by Participants in the Tragedy*. Glendale, Calif.: The Arthur H. Clark Co., 1960.

Jackson, Donald, and Mary Lee Spence. *The Expeditions of John Charles Frémont*, 3 vols. Urbana, Ill.: University of Illinois Press, 1970, 1973, 1984.

Nevins, Allan. *Frémont: Pathmaker of the West*. New York: Longmans, Green and Co., 1955.

Stegmaier, Mark J., and David H. Miller. *James F. Milligan: His Journal of Frémont's Fifth Expedition, 1853–1854; His Adventurous Life on Land and*

Sea. Glendale, Calif.: The Arthur H. Clark Co., 1988.

Gray, Robert

Howay, Frederic W., ed. *Voyages of the "Columbia" to the Northwest Coast 1787–1790 and 1790–1793.* Boston: The Massachusetts Historical Society, 1941.

Scofield, John. *Hail, Columbia: Robert Gray, John Kendrick and the Pacific Fur Trade.* Portland: Oregon Historical Society Press, 1993.

Vaughan, Thomas. "River of the West." *American History Illustrated* 27, no. 2 (May/June 1992): 28–43.

Long, Stephen Harriman

Benson, Maxine, ed. *From Pittsburgh to the Rocky Mountains: Major Stephen Long's Expedition 1819–1820.* Golden, Colo.: Fulcrum, Inc., 1988.

Fuller, Harlin M., and LeRoy R. Hafen, eds. "The Journal of Captain John R. Bell, Official Journalist For The Stephen H. Long Expedition To The Rocky Mountains, 1820." *The Far West and the Rockies Historical Series 1820–1875,* vol. 6. Glendale, Calif.: The Arthur H. Clark Co., 1957.

Nichols, Roger L., and Patrick L. Halley. *Stephen Long and American Frontier Exploration.* Norman, Okla.: University of Oklahoma Press, 1995.

Thwaites, Reuben Gold, ed. "Account of an Expedition From Pittsburgh To the Rocky Mountains, Performed in the Years 1819, 1820." Compiled by Edwin James. *Early Western Travels 1748–1846* vol. 14–17. Cleveland: The Arthur H. Clark Co., 1905.

Wood, Richard G. *Stephen Harriman Long 1784–1864: Army Engineer, Explorer, Inventor.* Glendale, Calif.: The Arthur H. Clark Co., 1966.

Mackenzie, Alexander

Gough, Barry. *First Across the Continent: Sir Alexander Mackenzie.* Norman, Okla.: University of Oklahoma Press, 1997.

Lamb, W. Kaye. "Sir Alexander Mackenzie." *Dictionary of Canadian Biography,* vol. 5. Toronto: University of Toronto Press, 1983.

———, ed. *The Journals and Letters of Sir Alexander Mackenzie (Voyages From Montreal, On The River St. Laurence, Through The Continent Of North America, To The Frozen And Pacific Oceans; In The Years 1789 and 1793 With A Preliminary Account Of The Rise, Progress, And Present State Of The Fur Trade Of That Country, by Alexander Mackenzie, Esq. 1801).* London: Cambridge University Press, 1970.

Tanner, Ogden. "The Epic Discoveries of a Fearless Scot." *The Canadians.* Alexandria, Va.: Time-Life Books, 1977.

Pike, Zebulon Montgomery

Hafen, LeRoy R. "Zebulon Montgomery Pike." *The Colorado Magazine* 8, no. 4 (July 1931): 132–142.

Hollon, W. Eugene. *The Lost Pathfinder: Zebulon Montgomery Pike.* Norman, Okla.: University of Oklahoma Press, 1949.

Jackson, Donald. "How Lost Was Pike?" *American Heritage* 16, no. 2 (February 1965): 10–14, 75–80.

———, ed. *The Journals of Zebulon Montgomery Pike with Letters and Related Documents,* 2 vols. Norman, Okla.: University of Oklahoma Press, 1966.

Pike, Zebulon Montgomery. *Exploratory Travels Through The Western Territories Of North America: Comprising A Voyage From St. Louis On The Mississippi, To The Source Of That River, And A Journey Through The Interior Of Louisiana And The North-Eastern Provinces Of New Spain.* London: Paternoster-Row, 1811. Reprint, Denver: W. H. Lawrence & Co., 1889.

Powell, John Wesley

Bartlett, Richard A. *Great Surveys of the American West.* Norman, Okla.: University of Oklahoma Press, 1962.

Darrah, William Culp. *Powell of the Colorado.* Princeton, N.J.: Princeton University Press, 1951.

———ed. "George Y. Bradley's Journal." *Utah Historical Quarterly* 15.

———. "J. C. Sumner's Journal." *Utah Historical Quarterly* 15.

———. "Journal of John F. Steward." *Utah Historical Quarterly* 16–17.

Dellenbaugh, Frederick S. *A Canyon Voyage: The Narrative Of The Second Powell Expedition Down The Green-Colorado River From Wyoming, And The Explorations On Land, In The Years 1871 and 1872.* New Haven, Conn.: Yale University Press, 1926.

Gregory, Dr. Herbert E., ed. "Journal of Stephen Vindiver Jones." *Utah Historical Quarterly* 16–17.

Hursch, Carolyn J. "Mapping the Colorado." *American History Magazine* 31, no. 3 (July/August 1996): 34–60.

John Wesley Powell: Soldier, Explorer, Scientist (booklet). U.S. Department of the Interior, Geological Survey, 1969.

Kelly, Charles, ed. "Capt. Francis Marion Bishop's Journal." *Utah Historical Quarterly* 15.

———. "Journal of W. C. Powell." *Utah Historical Quarterly* 16–17.

Lavender, David. "The Powell Expeditions [sic] First Conquest of the Colorado." *National Parks Magazine* 60, nos. 5–6 (May/June 1986): 16–21.

Powell, J. W. *The Exploration of the Colorado River and Its Canyons.* New York: Dover Publications, 1961.

Stegner, Wallace. *Beyond the Hundredth Meridian: John Wesley Powell and the Second Opening of the West.*

Boston: Houghton Mifflin, 1954.

Smith, Jedediah Strong

Brooks, George R., ed. *The Southwest Expedition of Jedediah S. Smith: His Personal Account of the Journey to California 1826–1827.* Glendale, Calif.: The Arthur H. Clark Co., 1977.

Carter, Harvey L. "Jedediah Smith." *The Mountain Men and the Fur Trade of the Far West,* vol. 8. Edited by LeRoy R. Hafen. Glendale, Calif.: The Arthur H. Clark Co., 1971.

Hafen, LeRoy R., and Ann W. Hafen. *Old Spanish Trail: Santa Fe to Los Angeles,* vol. 1. Glendale, Calif.: The Arthur H. Clark Co., 1954.

Morgan, Dale L. *Jedediah Smith and the Opening of the West.* Indianapolis: Bobbs-Merrill, 1953.

Sullivan, Maurice S. *The Travels of Jedediah Smith: A Documentary Outline Including the Journal of the Great American Pathfinder.* Lincoln, Nebr.: University of Nebraska Press, 1934, 1961.

Vancouver, George

Anderson, Bern. *Surveyor of the Sea: The Life and Voyages of Captain George Vancouver.* Seattle: University of Washington Press, 1960.

Godwin, George. *Vancouver: A Life 1757–1798.* New York: D. Appleton and Company, 1931.

Lamb, W. Kaye. "George Vancouver." *Dictionary of Canadian Biography,* vol. 4. Toronto: University of Toronto Press, 1979.

——, ed. *George Vancouver: A Voyage of Discovery to the North Pacific Ocean and Round the World 1791–1795,* 4 vols. London: The Hakluyt Society, 1984.

Walker, Joseph Reddeford

Booth, Percy H. "West Wind: The Life of Joseph Reddeford Walker." Reprinted in *Old West* 3, no. 2 (winter 1966): 72–96.

Conner, Daniel Ellis. *Joseph Reddeford Walker and the Arizona Adventure.* Edited by Donald J. Berthrong and Odessa Davenport. Norman, Okla.: University of Oklahoma Press, 1956.

Ewers, John C., ed. *Adventures of Zenas Leonard.* Norman, Okla.: University of Oklahoma Press, 1959.

Gilbert, Bil. *Westering Man: The Life of Joseph Walker, Master of the Frontier.* New York: Atheneum, 1983.

Lauderdale, Beverly. "Camped in Yosemite: Captain Joseph Reddeford Walker." *True West* 40, no. 10 (October 1993): 46–51.

Lovell, Merton N. "Joseph R. Walker: Mountain Man and Guide of the Far West." Master's thesis, Brigham Young University, Provo, Utah, June 1959.

Walker, Ardis M. "Joseph R. Walker." *The Mountain Men and the Fur Trade of the Far West,* vol. 5. Edited by LeRoy R. Hafen. Glendale, Calif.: The Arthur H. Clark Co., 1968.

TIME LINE

754
* The French and Indian War begins

1755
* Robert Gray is born

1757
* George Vancouver is born

1764
* Alexander Mackenzie is born

1773
* The first schoolhouse west of the Allegheny Mountains is completed
* Colonists dump tea into harbor during Boston Tea Party

1774 or 1775
* John Colter is born

1775
* First shots are fired in the Revolutionary War
* Paul Revere makes his famous midnight ride

1776
* Declaration of Independence is signed

1777
* The first American flag is formally adopted in Philadelphia

1779
* John Paul Jones defeats the British on the high seas
* Zebulon M. Pike is born

1784
* Stephen H. Long is born

1786
* The first Indian reservation is established

1787
* Delaware is the first state admitted to the Union
* The Constitutional Convention meets to write the United States Constitution
* Robert Gray leaves on his first expedition

1789
* George Washington is inaugurated as the first president of the United States
* Alexander Mackenzie leads his first expedition to explore the river now known as the Mackenzie River

1790
✳Robert Gray is captain of the first American ship to carry the United States flag around the world
✳ Robert Gray leaves on his second expedition

1792
✳George Vancouver reaches the northwest coast of North America to search for the Northwest Passage

1792–1793
✳Robert Gray discovers the Columbia River

1793
✳Eli Whitney invents the cotton gin
✳Alexander Mackenzie leads his second expedition and becomes the first European American to cross the North American continent north of Mexico
✳George Vancouver returns to the northwest coast of North America and explores the coasts of British Columbia and Alaska

1794
✳George Vancouver returns to the Alaskan coast
✳Charles Willson Peale opens the first United States Museum in Philadelphia

1795
✳Edward Jenner makes the first successful

smallpox vaccination

1797
✳John Adams is inaugurated as the second president of the United States

1798
✳George Vancouver dies
✳Joseph R. Walker is born

1799
✳George Washington dies
✳Jedediah S. Smith is born

1800
✳The Library of Congress is established
✳Washington, D.C. becomes the nation's capital

1801
✳Thomas Jefferson is inaugurated as the third president of the United States

1803
✳The United States purchases Louisiana Territory

1804
✳The Lewis and Clark Expedition (the Corps of Discovery) leaves St. Louis
✳Jim Bridger is born

1805–1806
✳Zebulon M. Pike makes his first

expedition to the upper Mississippi
River

1806
✷The Lewis and Clark Expedition returns
to St. Louis
✷Noah Webster publishes America's first
dictionary
✷Robert Gray dies

1806–1807
✷Zebulon M. Pike leads his second
expedition to present-day
southwestern United States

1807
✷Robert Fulton's steamboat is launched

1807–1809
✷John Colter makes his historic 500-mile
trek and is the first white man to
explore much of today's Wyoming

1809
✷James Madison is inaugurated as the
fourth president of the United States

1811
✷The first colonists reach the coast of
what will become Oregon

1812
✷The United States declares war on Great
Britain, beginning the War of 1812

1813
✷John Colter dies
✷Zebulon M. Pike dies
✷John C. Frémont is born

1815
✷The first railroad track is laid in the
United States

1817
✷James Monroe is inaugurated as the fifth
president of the United States
✷Stephen H. Long makes his first
expedition to what is now Minnesota
and Wisconsin

1819–1820
✷Stephen H. Long's second expedition
takes his steamboat *Western Engineer*
up the Missouri River, and then goes
overland as far west as present-day
Colorado and New Mexico

1820
✷The Missouri Compromise bans slavery
west of the Mississippi River
✷Alexander Mackenzie dies

1823
✷The Erie Canal is completed
✷Stephen H. Long leads his third
expedition as far north as
Canada

1823–1826
✷Jedediah S. Smith leads a trapping party

through Montana, Idaho, Utah, and
Wyoming

1824
✳ Jedediah S. Smith discovers South Pass
✳ Jim Bridger discovers Great Salt Lake

1825
✳ John Quincy Adams is inaugurated as the
   sixth president of the United States
✳ Jim Bridger explores much of today's
   Yellowstone National Park

1826–1827
✳ Jedediah S. Smith leads an expedition and
   becomes the first European-American
   to go overland into California

1827–1829
✳ Jedediah S. Smith leads a second
   expedition to California and overland
   to Oregon

1829
✳ Andrew Jackson is inaugurated as the
   seventh president of the United
   States
✳ Congress authorizes the Indian Removal
   Act

1831
✳ Jedediah S. Smith dies

1832
✳ The Black Hawk War begins

✳ Henry R. Schoolcraft discovers the true
   source of the Mississippi River

1833–1834
✳ Joseph R. Walker leads an expedition to
   California over the Sierra Nevada and
   discovers Yosemite Valley and the
   giant redwood trees

1834
✳ John W. Powell is born

1836
✳ The Alamo falls

1837
✳ Martin Van Buren is inaugurated as the
   eighth president of the United States

1838
✳ The Cherokees are forced to move to
   Oklahoma along the Trail of Tears

1840
✳ American Lieutenant Charles Wilkes
   sights Antarctica

1841
✳ The first wagon train leaves Independence,
   Missouri, for California
✳ William Henry Harrison is inaugurated as
   the ninth president of the United
   States, but dies one month later
✳ John Tyler is inaugurated as the tenth
   president of the United States

1842
✱ John C. Frémont leads his first expedition to the Rocky Mountains

1843
✱ More than 1,000 settlers leave Independence, Missouri, for Oregon
✱ Joseph R. Walker guides the first emigrants into California over the California Trail

1843–1844
✱ John C. Frémont leads his second expedition to Oregon and California

1844
✱ John Tyler is the first American president to marry while in office
✱ The first message is sent over a telegraph line

1845
✱ James Knox Polk is inaugurated as the eleventh president of the United States

1845–1846
✱ John C. Frémont leads his third expedition to California and becomes involved in the war with Mexico

1846
✱ The Mexican War begins

1848
✱ Gold is found in California, setting off the gold rush

1848–1849
✱ John C. Frémont leads his fourth expedition to the southern Colorado mountains and eventually to California

1849
✱ Zachary Taylor is inaugurated as the twelfth president of the United States

1850
✱ Millard Fillmore is inaugurated as the thirteenth president of the United States
✱ Levi Strauss begins manufacturing blue jeans
✱ Jim Bridger guides Captain Stansbury through Bridger's Pass

1851
✱ Herman Melville publishes *Moby Dick*

1853
✱ Franklin Pierce is inaugurated as the fourteenth president of the United States
✱ The United States buys what will become parts of Arizona and New Mexico

1853–1854
✱ John C. Frémont leads his fifth expedition through Colorado, Utah, and on to California

1857
✱ The Supreme Court decrees that no black

person can be a United States citizen
❋James Buchanan is inaugurated as the
fifteenth president of the United States

1858

❋Julia Archibald Holmes is the first
woman to climb Pikes Peak
❋Abraham Lincoln and Stephen Douglas
debate the slavery issue

1860

❋The first Pony Express rider leaves St.
Joseph, Missouri

1861

❋Abraham Lincoln is inaugurated as the
sixteenth president of the United
States
❋The Civil War begins in Fort Sumter,
South Carolina

1863

❋President Lincoln issues the
Emancipation Proclamation
❋President Lincoln delivers the
Gettysburg Address

1864

❋Stephen H. Long dies

1865

❋Abraham Lincoln is assassinated
❋The Civil War ends
❋Andrew Johnson is inaugurated as the
seventeenth president of the United
States

1866

❋Red Cloud's War of 1866–1868 begins

1867

❋The United States buys Alaska from
Russia for $7.2 million
❋Jim Bridger guides the Carrington
Expedition from Fort Keary,
Nebraska to Virginia City,
Montana

1869

❋The Golden Spike is driven at
Promontory Point, Utah, connecting
railroads from the East Coast to the
West Coast
❋Ulysses S. Grant is inaugurated as the
eighteenth president of the United
States
❋Women win the vote in Wyoming
❋John W. Powell leads his first expedition
down the Green and Colorado rivers
and through the Grand Canyon

1871

❋The Great Fire burns Chicago

1871–1872

❋John W. Powell leads his second
expedition down the Green and
Colorado rivers and through the
Grand Canyon

1872

❋The Modoc War of 1872–1873 begins
❋Billy Hawkins and Andy Hall run the last

boat from the Powell Expedition to
the Gulf of Mexico

1874
✶The Kiowa-Comanche War of 1874–1875
begins

1875
✶The Sioux War of 1875–1877 begins

1876
✶The telephone is patented
✶Joseph R. Walker dies

1877
✶The Nez Percé War of 1877 begins
✶Rutherford B. Hayes is inaugurated as the
nineteenth president of the United
States

1878
✶The Bannock War of 1878 begins

1879
✶The Ute War of 1879–1880 begins

1880
✶The Apache War of the 1880s begins

1881
✶James A. Garfield is inaugurated as the
twentieth president of the United
States
✶Chester Alan Arthur is inaugurated as the
twenty-first president of the United
States
✶Jim Bridger dies

1885
✶Grover Cleveland is inaugurated as the
twenty-second president of the
United States

1890
✶The last battle of the Plains Indian Wars
is fought in December between the
Sioux and the U.S. Army at Wounded
Knee, South Dakota
✶John C. Frémont dies

1902
✶John W. Powell dies

ILLUSTRATION CREDITS

We apologize for any unintentional omissions and will be pleased to correct
any inadvertent errors or omissions in future editions.

American Philosophical Society, Philadelphia,
Pennsylvania: p. 57

Clymer Museum of Art, Ellensburg,
Washington: p. 47

Courtesy, Colorado State Historical Society: p.
61

Courtesy of Columbia River Maritime Museum,
Astoria, Oregon: pp. 14, 16, and 18

Cosmopolitan Magazine (August 1896): p. 159

Denver Public Library, Western History
Collection: pp. 33, 60, 96, 110, 146, 147, 151,
and 153

Courtesy of Grand Canyon National Park
Museum: pp. ii (17262) and 178 (17262)

Independence National Historical Park, Philadelphia, Pennsylvania: pp. 56 and 69

Joslyn Art Museum, Omaha, Nebraska: pp. 97
and 130

Library of Congress: pp. 7, 22, 23, 46, 48, 64, 71,
72, 73, 75, 79, 84, 86, 99, 105, 125, 127, 135,
136, 140, 141, 142, 152, 157, 158, 161, 165, 180,
and 196

National Archives and Records Administration:
pp. 51 and 186

National Archives of Canada: pp. 6 (detail from
C011226), 12 (C150721), 26 (detail from
C069199), 35 (detail from C002390), 42
(detail from C003130), 66 (C002935), 82
(detail from C017338), and 107 (top,
C000421); William Armstrong: p. 36
(detail from C019041); George Back: p. 31

(detail from C093021); Frances Anne Hop-
kins: pp. 34 (detail from C013585), 39
(C002772), and 40 (detail from C002773);
Harry Humphrys: p. 25 (detail from
C095848); and Rogers: p. 37 (detail from
C016859)

National Park Service: pp. 95, 106, 108, 122, and 128

National Park Service, Scotts Bluff National
Historic Site, Scottsbluff, Nebraska: p. 85

National Park Service, Yellowstone National
Park, Wyoming: p. 53

Nebraska State Historical Society: p. 70

Oregon Legislative Administration, Information
Systems: p. 11

U.S. Geological Survey: J. K. Hiller: pp. 109
(detail), 183, 184 (detail), 185 (detail), 189
(detail), 191 (detail), 192, 193 (detail), 197
(detail), and 198 (detail); J. P. Iddings: p. 94;
Portraits 2: p. 168 (detail)

Used by permission, Utah State Historical
Society, all rights reserved: pp. 87, 90, 92,
104 , 117, 119, 131, 138, 164, 170, 171, 174, and
176

Vancouver Public Library, Special Collections:
pp. 9 (detail from 8036), 20 (detail from
7895), 24 (7998), and 29 (detail from 8039)

Wyoming Game and Fish Department: p. 83

Wyoming State Archives, Wyoming Division of
Cultural Resources: p. 98 (detail)

Yosemite Museum, Yosemite, California: pp. 124
and 126

INDEX

Page numbers in *italics* refer to illustrations and maps.